WINNING GYMNASTICS FOR GIRLS

WINNING GYMNASTICS FOR GIRLS

DAVID PORTER

Foreword by
DAVID A. FEIGLEY, Ph.D.
Chair, Department of Exercise Science and Sports Studies, Rutgers University

A MOUNTAIN LION BOOK

Facts On File, Inc.

WINNING GYMNASTICS FOR GIRLS

Facts On File, Inc.
132 West 31st Street
New York NY 10001

Library of Congress Cataloging-in-Publication Data

Porter, David, 1960–.
Winning gymnastics for girls / David Porter ; foreword by David A. Feigley.
p. cm. — (Winning sports for girls)
"A Mountain Lion book."
ISBN 0-8160-5229-8 (HC : alk. paper)
1. Gymnastics for girls—Juvenile literature. I. Title. II. Series.
GV464.P65 2003 2003014767

Facts On File books are available at special discounts when purchased in bulk quantities for businesses, associations, institutions, or sales promotions. Please call our Special Sales Department in New York at (212) 967-8800 or (800) 322-8755.

You can find Facts On File on the World Wide Web at http://www.factsonfile.com

Text design by Erika K. Arroyo
Cover design by Nora Wertz

Printed in the United States of America

VB FOF 10 9 8 7 6 5 4 3 2 1

This book is printed on acid-free paper.

CONTENTS

FOREWORD

I married into gymnastics. Let me explain.

I grew up in Lancaster, Pennsylvania, playing soccer and competing in springboard diving and swimming. I captained my high school swimming and diving team at McCaskey High School and my college swimming and diving team at Rutgers University in New Brunswick, New Jersey. After graduating from college, I coached diving at Somerset Valley YMCA in Somerville, New Jersey. Diving is a sport similar to gymnastics in that it involves somersaulting and twisting but quite different in that landing in water requires much less skill than landing on the floor, even though the floor is padded with firm landing mats.

The YMCA where I coached diving also hosted the practices of a local high school girls' gymnastics team. My team and the gymnastics team shared a gym and a trampoline with an overhead spotting rig. A very attractive woman coached the gymnastics team. Eventually she agreed to go out on a date with me, and several years later she agreed to marriage.

Unfortunately, during our first year of marriage we hardly saw each other. She coached gymnastics before school, early in the morning; taught physical education during the schoolday; coached the high school gymnastics team after school; and then coached a youth sports gymnastics team until late in the evening. I attended graduate school during the day and then coached diving five hours per day at the YMCA (a program that produced international competitors). After a year of this madness, we decided that I would change sports and coach gymnastics so my wife and I could work together. That decision led me into women's gymnastics, a sport characterized by beauty, elegance, and an incredible work ethic.

I now realize that gymnastics would have helped me as an athlete to be successful in any sport. Physically, it teaches balance, grace, strength, flexibility, and cardiovascular conditioning. Mentally, it teaches focus, concentration, overcoming fear, determination, and the drive to "stick to it" until mastering a skill. Gymnastics combines the elements of dance with the explosive power of tumbling and requires superb physical conditioning and sharp mental skills. In addition, it allows gymnasts to contribute to the success of a team while relying on individual accomplishment. It is a power sport that emphasizes the beauty of the human body as well as technical skills needed to overcome gravity.

Gymnastics has a niche for every athlete. Whether you are a recreational athlete doing gymnastics once a week or a highly competitive gymnast training every day for major competitions, gymnastics can offer an appropriate challenge (from "Can I master that move?" to "Can I score a 9.0?"). In gymnastics, as you gain control over your movements, your self-confidence grows. And one of the things I love about the sport is that you don't have to be the best to be successful. Mastering a forward roll by a beginner or learning a back walkover by an intermediate can be just as exciting as learning a double back somersault by an advanced athlete. Overcoming the butterflies in your stomach and learning first to complete the skill and then to execute it with certain flair are building blocks for being a successful gymnast and a successful person.

Some young athletes learn quickly while others progress more slowly, but all can master the basic skills of artistic gymnastics if they are willing to keep at it and master the prerequisites, which are strength and flexibility. The results produce not only success at gymnastics but also a healthy body and a positive mental approach that easily transfers to other areas of your life, such as school, work, and family. In *Winning Gymnastics for Girls,* David Porter's vivid descriptions and photographs of youngsters performing basic gymnastic skills are certain to capture the interest of many girls. His guidelines for a safe learning environment and tips for selecting appropriate gymnastic schools and qualified instructors are valuable pieces of information to help parents provide their young daughters with a quality youth sports experience.

—David A. Feigley, Ph.D.
Chair, Department of Exercise, Science, and Sports Studies
Rutgers University

ACKNOWLEDGMENTS

This book was developed and produced by Mountain Lion, Inc., a book producer specializing in instructional and general reference sports books. A book producer relies on the skills of many people who contribute their special talents and efforts. To all of them, thank you for a job well done:

- David Porter, who wrote the text, and James Chambers, editor at Facts On File, who shepherded the project from start to finish
- Drew Schwartz and Caitlin Kelly, who researched and contributed portions of the text, including the history of gymnastics (Drew) and history of rhythmic gymnastics (Caitlin)
- David A. Feigley, Ph.D., who contributed the foreword, vetted the technical accuracy of the stunt and skill descriptions, and guided us to a venue for the photography
- Gymnastics instructor Matt Deibert, managers Karen Brooks and Trish Sutphen, and instructors Lynn Pachanski and Salvatore Macaro of Feigley's Gymnastics in South Plainfield, New Jersey, who answered all our questions about gymnastics and provided invaluable assistance during the photography session
- Jeanine Summers, coach of the Jersey Gemz, the terrific and skillful cheerleaders who demonstrated many of their stunts
- Gymnasts Sarah Brooks, Shannon Bell, and Rachel Zickert, who ably and cheerfully demonstrated all their accomplished skills on the floor, balance beam, vault, and uneven bars
- Beverly Schaefer, who captured on film all the important skills, stunts, and maneuvers that make up the exciting sport of gymnastics
- Wes Marutani of Arena Gymnastics in Princeton, New Jersey, who provided valuable information for the Parents and Tots section

INTRODUCTION

This book is for any young girl who wants to learn about the wide range of gymnastics skills and how to do them. The sport of gymnastics is ever expanding, and it offers girls exciting events of all types. From floor exercises to cheerleading and rhythmic gymnastics, the skills of gymnastics bring out the power, beauty, and grace that embody what has been called the purest sport.

In gymnastics the athlete first masters basic skills and then uses her mastery to learn more advanced techniques and maneuvers. For example, aspiring gymnasts must first learn to perform a handstand head balance before trying a handstand and a cartwheel before attempting a one-handed cartwheel. The chapters of *Winning Gymnastics for Girls* follow this progression from learning basic skills to building on these skills with advanced techniques and maneuvers.

Almost all gymnastics skills are derived from what are essentially basic human movements. Activities such as running, jumping, rolling over, climbing, and swinging, for instance, come naturally to all of us. They are also the main building blocks of gymnastics. *Winning Gymnastics for Girls* will help you learn the basics of these movements, and your success may even inspire you to refine them and eventually raise your efforts to the highest standards of the sport, that of Olympic competition. But even at the highest levels of competition that feature the most advanced gymnastics routines, you will recognize movements that children can do almost instinctively.

This means that right from the start, without ever having been formally introduced to the sport, you have probably had some gymnastics experience. You may not yet know how to swing on uneven bars or make a dismount, but chances are you have some idea of the kind of strength and control these moves require. Remember that pole you climbed, jungle gym bar you swung from, or curb you walked along? Your familiarity makes it that much easier to appreciate gymnastics maneuvers and stunts and to imagine how much fun it would be to do them.

With gymnastics you're in for not only a lot of fun but also loads of personal growth. Gymnastics is a sport that transforms individuals into powerful and confident athletes. It may surprise you, but gymnastics is a sport for all shapes and sizes of individuals. Gymnastics builds a superb body and instills quiet confidence among its practitioners. As you work the apparatus, your body will build itself naturally. You should apply the conditioning exercises presented in this book, but most of your strength, power, balance, and agility will be derived from performing the actual activities. As you become stronger and able to perform more and more stunts, your confidence builds until nothing will seem impossible.

Sections of this book dealing with floor exercises, the uneven bars, the balance beam, vaulting, the trampoline, cheerleading, and rhythmic gymnastics should be read, thought about, tried, and practiced, and then reread. By returning to the text and photographs for further study, you will eventually internalize the proper mechanics of the various stunts and maneuvers.

Practice correctly and often. Ask a friend, a parent, or your gymnastics coach to critique your technique and style. It may take awhile to learn, but once you perform a stunt successfully, the feeling of satisfaction you get is tremendous. Once you've mastered one stunt, you will want to go back and do it a little better. Then you'll want to move on to another stunt to master. Gymnastics can hook you for life, but there's no danger with this addiction—it's a healthy and productive endeavor that brings no harm, only much joy and satisfaction.

1 HISTORY

THE ORIGINS OF GYMNASTICS

Picture yourself in a time machine that takes you back 35,000 or 40,000 years ago, to the beginning of modern humanity. You are about to see how humans' first movements led to gymnastics.

Your oldest ancestors, the Cro-Magnons, stand before you. They slightly resemble you, but you barely recognize them. They stand about three feet tall; hair covers their face and body. They speak, but you can't understand them. Silently, you wonder what exactly is "modern" about the Cro-Magnons.

Things look more like Jurassic Park than the park in your neighborhood. Welcome to the jungle. Animals large and small, from lions to lizards, are all around. Swamps, streams, and rivers surround you. A rhinoceros charges the leader of your group, who picks up a stone weapon, jumps onto the animal to jab it, and vaults to safety. Others in the group swing onto a tree branch or perform a tumbling trick to get out of the way. The rhino runs away, but the leader lets everyone know more may be on the way. Logs form a path across the stream to safety.

Our earliest ancestors used basic gymnastics skills to help them survive. They swung from trees, vaulted, and tumbled to avoid charging bulls, buffaloes, and other beasts. They balanced themselves on logs to walk across rivers and streams.

Thousands of years before gymnastics became a competitive sport, ancient civilizations practiced and celebrated some of its most basic skills. More than 5,000 years ago, Egyptian acrobats entertained audiences. Most of these acrobats were women, and paintings of their performances were eventually discovered in tombs. Hieroglyphics and other records suggest that people in ancient China and India also performed tumbling and balancing.

The Minoans, who were named after King Minos, ruled the Mediterranean Sea from about 2500 to 1500 B.C. They lived on the island of Crete (near modern Greece) and trained young men and women to tumble, balance, and vault. These athletes risked their lives by trying to leap over bulls at the palace of King Minos. With a running start, they would try to grab a charging bull's horns, vault into the air by kicking their feet over their head, land on the bull's back, and then dismount by jumping to safety behind its tail. The bull was a symbol of power to Minoans, and as many as 5,000 people came to the king's palace at Knossos to watch these contests.

One wrong move could cause death. Obviously, this was a quantum leap away from present-day gymnastics, but the Minoans started their bull-leaping routine with a front handspring. Without the bull, of course, the front handspring is still used today. The Minoans were great artists and left proof of their tumbling skills. Archaeologists discovered drawings of athletes vaulting over bulls on the palace walls of Knossos.

A few centuries after these daredevils vaulted into the air, the people of ancient Greece gave us a name for the sport. *Gymnastics* comes from the Greek word *gymnos,* which means "naked." The Greeks built large public gymnasiums without roofs and called them *gymnos.* They were the first society to believe that developing the body and mind would make a person healthy and well. Citizens exercised without clothes and then went to other areas of the gymnasium to learn.

Physical fitness was part of the daily routine for males in ancient Greece; only boys and men were allowed to attend the gymnasiums. They removed their clothes, smeared olive oil on their bodies, and worked out by running sprints, lifting weights and jumping with them, throwing the discus and javelin, wrestling, and boxing. The Greeks designed different types of physical activity to achieve specific goals. These systems of exercise became known as gymnastics. But none of the training programs included skills that are used in modern gymnastics. Ordinary citizens exercised to achieve physical fitness. In the city-state of Sparta, soldiers trained to increase their strength and toughness for battle. The best athletes had a special exercise program to prepare for the Olympic Games.

At first each of the city-states held their own games. The Greeks loved athletic competition, and eventually the games spread throughout the peninsula. The first Olympic Games were held in Athens on Mount Olympus in 776 B.C., after which they were held every four years. The pentathlon was the heart of the ancient Olympics, but gymnastics was not included in its five events. Athletes raced in the 200-yard dash, competed in the broad jump, threw the discus and javelin, and wrestled.

Gymnasiums nearly disappeared during the time of the Roman Empire. Although a student of medicine named Claudius Galen lectured and wrote about the benefits of gymnastics, his advice was largely ignored. Ordinary citizens did not exercise, but the Roman armies did use gymnastics to train their soldiers, practicing mounts and dismounts on wooden horses. Almost 2,000 years later, the first vaulting equipment in modern gymnastics looked much like a horse; it was made of wood, and one end curved upward like a horse's neck while the other end had a tail. Of course, they called it a horse.

In ancient Rome, exercise and games were thought to be immoral and useless. Christianity then spread throughout the empire, and many people believed that Satan lived in the body. This belief gained credibility as the Olympics became more corrupt. The Christian emperor Theodosius abolished the Olympic Games in A.D. 393. Gymnastics had entered the dark ages and exited the world's stage for more than 1,000 years. It would reappear in a more recognizable form in the early 1800s, when modern gymnastics began to take shape. In the meantime, acrobats and dancers used tumbling skills that would become part of the sport and add to the rich history of gymnastics.

During the Middle Ages, traveling minstrel groups told stories through song, accompanied by the harp or a bagpipe, and performed tumbling for knights and others. These professional minstrels, who lived on the road, took their money and moved on to the next village or household. The minstrels separated themselves from the social structure of the villages they visited so they never had to fear the disapproval of religious or civil authorities.

The French medieval tale of a minstrel who became a monk, called "The Tumbler of Our Lady," was written in the 13th century and is still popular. The uneducated protagonist could not speak well enough to join in the prayers at the monastery of Clairvaux. As the story describes, "He had lived only to tumble, to turn somersaults, to spring, and to dance. To leap and to jump, this he knew but naught else." So he worshiped Our Lady the only way he could.

Whenever the bell rang for Mass, he would sneak down to the crypt, take off his habit, and perform a spectacular routine of somersaults and handstands. Eventually, one of the monks saw the tumbler and reported this to the abbot. Together, they secretly watched the tumbler perform and were amazed. Covered with sweat "as the grease issues from spitted meat," the tumbler collapsed from heat exhaustion. But an angel sent by Our Lady revived him. The abbot had great respect for the tumbler. When the tumbler died, the monks and the abbot saw that the Holy Mother and the angels protected him. Thereafter, tumblers were considered specially blessed.

Women performed gymnastics moves to music, as they do today in modern floor exercises. In England, Matilda Makejoy entertained King Edward I and his court for 14 years during his reign from 1272 to 1307. Balancing became very popular in the 1300s; women steadied themselves on the edge of a rolling tambourine. King Henry VIII paid the daughter of one of his jugglers to do tumbling in celebration of the birth of his natural son in 1519.

An acrobat named S. A. Tuccaro wrote a book about jumping and tumbling that was published in Paris in 1589. *Three Dialogues on the Art of Tumbling and Jumping in the Air* had many illustrations for its time. Certainly gymnasts were inspired by it, and acrobatics are a major part of today's floor exercise.

It is fitting that gymnastics started to come out of the shadows during the Enlightenment in the 18th century. Even before this time, the philosophers Montaigne (16th century) and John Locke (17th century) wrote that exercise should be part of education. In the 1700s the French philosopher Jean-Jacques Rousseau also believed that physical activities would improve the quality of education for young people. Back then, gymnastics and physical education were considered the same thing. Rousseau's book on education reform influenced the development of modern gymnastics, and later on, his writing helped inspire the French Revolution.

A German teacher named Johann Friedrich Guts Muths used some of Rousseau's ideas to develop a physical education program incorporating 11 types of exercises. His students practiced balancing by walking on large logs. Back then, only boys and young men participated in physical education classes. But Guts Muths was ahead of his time. His book, *Gymnastics for the Young,* published in 1793, described exercises for girls and had a great impact on physical education for many years. It was translated into French, English, Swedish, and Danish.

Friedrich Ludwig Jahn opened the first gymnastics center near Berlin in 1811. His students practiced outdoors, at an open-air gymnasium called a *Turnplatz.* Jahn invented the parallel bars, rings, and high bar and is known as the father of modern gymnastics. He developed exercises for his students to swing on a wooden horse, which he called a *Swingel.* Jahn used two curved wooden pommels as handles, and that's how it became known as the pommel horse. Many of the moves that his students practiced are still used in modern men's competition.

Jahn lived in the German state of Prussia, which was under Napoleon Bonaparte's rule for many years. Jahn was very devoted to gymnastics because he wanted to make the people in his country physically strong for war. In 1813, Jahn and his followers, called the Turners, began a two-year fight for independence against Napoleon, and after the battle of Waterloo, Prussia became an independent state. The German word *turnen* means to "perform gymnastics exercises," and the Turners were committed to the growth of gymnastics.

The German gymnastics movement stalled in 1819 when Jahn was accused of treason and went to jail for a year. In 1820, the Prussian government banned gymnastics and Jahn remained under house arrest for five years. Until 1840, when King Frederick William IV took the throne, gymnastics had to be practiced secretly. During this time, three of Jahn's followers feared they would be persecuted in Prussia because of their political beliefs and came to the United States. One of these men, Charles Beck was now free to become this country's first gymnastics teacher at the Round Hill School in Northampton, Massachusetts.

The founders of the Round Hill School learned about the Turners' gymnastics program while studying in Germany. Returning home, they decided to start the first required physical education program in the United States. In 1825, they hired German immigrant Charles Beck, who taught gymnastics to the students. Of the other Turners who emigrated, Charles Follen taught German at Harvard University, introduced Jahn's gymnastics to his students, and also taught gymnastics at a public gymnasium that he opened in Boston. Francis Lieber, who briefly took over the Boston gymnasium, became a professor and well-known political theorist who gave advice to the Union government during the Civil War.

Meanwhile, Per Henrik Ling of Sweden created another type of gymnastics designed to improve health. It became known as Swedish gymnastics, and some even called it medical gymnastics. But Ling, like his German counterpart Jahn, wanted to use gymnastics to train the military, whereas the followers of Jahn and Ling created an artistic form of gymnastics that could be used for the general population. Through the years, artistic gymnastics has changed, of course, but it is still the main branch of gymnastics.

Ling's gymnastics focused on precise body positions while his rival, Jahn, emphasized strength. This difference meant that Ling's system could be taught to women. The movements on Ling's apparatus, such as the balance beam, window ladder, and Swedish box, did not require great physical strength, but each exercise was designed to achieve a specific benefit. The instructors made sure that students held all of the correct body positions. Years later, Ling's followers allowed their students to move more freely. This led to the development of modern floor exercises.

Ling's followers introduced this system in other Scandinavian countries, such as Denmark, Finland, and Norway. For the first time, girls and women got the chance to participate in gymnastics. Swedish gymnastics also caught on in England. In the late 1800s it was even taught to British girls in nursery schools. American women received their first gymnastics instruction at Mount Holyoke College in 1862.

During this time gymnastics became popular throughout Europe. Heinrich Clias, who was born in the United States, established gymnastics programs in Switzerland, England, and France. Gymnastics was also introduced in Italy, Poland, Holland, and Russia.

Many of these countries decided to form a gymnastics organization in 1881. The Federation of International Gymnastics (FIG) is the oldest international sports group and still sets the rules for international gymnastics competition. At the time of its foundation, it was called the European Gymnastics Federation and helped ensure that gymnastics was one of the nine sports in the first modern Olympic Games, which were held in Athens, Greece, in 1896. For the historic event workers restored the ancient Olympic Stadium in Athens, which had not been used for 2,000 years.

Many things have changed since the first Olympic gymnastics competition. Women waited more than 50 years, until the 1952 Olympics, to compete in individual gymnastics events, and only in the 1928 Olympics did women compete as a team in different gymnastics events for the first time. The Dutch women's gymnastics team won the first gold medal.

In the 1896 games, any male athlete who showed up could compete in the five gymnastics events: parallel bars, high bar, pommel horse, vault, and rings. Four years later, Olympics organizers combined track and field events with gymnastics.

It took many years for gymnastics to break away from track and field. The ninth gymnastics world championship in 1930 held events in the pole vault, broad jump, shot put, rope climb, and 100-meter dash. After that gymnastics started to eliminate track and field events and turned in a different direction. By the 1952 Olympics, gymnastics had separated itself completely.

Gymnastics went through growing pains, and international competition outside the Olympics helped the sport form its own identity. Only four countries—Belgium, France, Luxembourg, and Holland—participated in the first world championship of gymnastics held in Belgium in 1903. Teams often brought their own apparatus to the events. One gymnast dislocated his finger and held his position on the parallel bars while it was reset. The rules back then allowed him to repeat the exercise.

FIG brought about major changes in gymnastics, gained power when it took control of Olympic gymnastic events, and decided to hold the world championships every four years between the Olympics. At the 1924 Olympics, FIG established individual competitions for each of the apparatus, as well as in combined individual and team exercises. Women gymnasts got their first chance to compete in combined team exercises in the 1928 Olympics. Four years later, FIG introduced floor exercises to the Olympics, but women gymnasts did not compete in the 1932 Los Angeles Games. The U.S. women's gymnastics team first competed in the 1936 Olympics, which were held in Berlin.

National gymnastics organizations sprouted up to help many countries prepare for international competition. In the United States the YMCA, American Turners, and Sokols began holding gymnastics competitions for their members in the early 1900s. The Amateur Athletic Union (AAU) sponsored open gymnastics contests for many years.

As gymnastics became more popular, the United States Gymnastics Federation (later USA Gymnastics) began organizing gymnastics competition. During the mid-1960s, 7,000 athletes competed in gymnastics. In 1970 USA Gymnastics became the national governing body of all gymnastics organizations in the country. Presently, USA Gymnastics selects and trains the gymnastics teams for the Olympics and world championships, and more than 70,000 athletes are registered with USA Gymnastics. Each year, USA Gymnastics holds more than 3,000 competitions and has more than 13,000 professional and instructor members.

Gymnastics had undergone a major face-lift, which was first noticed at the 1952 Olympics. For the first time individual female gymnasts could prance with pride during the floor exercise, and for the first time women competed individually, as a team, and in all-around competition on the balance beam, vault, and uneven bars. This format is still used today.

In 1952 big breakthroughs were about to happen. Women finally had equal opportunity to show their skills. The world would see the grace and glamour of women's gymnastics.

EQUIPMENT

Gymnastics is the only major sport with equipment specifically designed for women. The balance beam and the uneven bars are not used in men's gymnastics. Both women and men compete in the floor exercise and vaulting, but there are obvious differences in their grace and strength. For example, women dance to music that they choose as part of their floor routine. A quick rundown on the history of each event follows.

Balance Beam

Long before the first piece of gymnastics equipment was invented, French soldiers practiced balancing on large logs. Friedrich Jahn called his perfectly round balance logs *Schweben,* the German word for "floating." Students of Ling's gymnastics used the lower part of the Swedish bench to develop their balancing skills. The Swedish beam became a popular training tool in women's gymnastics all over the world, but it was too low and narrow to be used in gymnastics competition.

Women gymnasts began competing on the balance beam at the world championships of gymnastics in 1934. Held in Budapest, Hungary, it was also the first time women competed in individual gymnastics events. Gaki Meszaros from Hungary performed a split on the beam that set a spectacular standard for the time. The beam was about an inch narrower, or eight centimeters wide, than it is at present.

Women gymnasts wanted firmer footing and safer conditions to perform dazzling moves on the beam, and the rule makers agreed. The beam was widened about an inch, to today's standard of 10 centimeters, and the sides of the beam were slightly rounded. Two inner support stands were added in 1965 to stabilize the beam.

In the 1970s Olympic athletes began doing flips and handsprings on the balance beam. A combination of foam rubber and plywood replaced the hard wood surface on the top of the beam and underneath it. With today's thick protective padding, preteens safely perform somersaults on the balance beam.

Vaulting

The life-threatening risk of vaulting basically disappeared when the ancient Minoans stopped doing handsprings over a bull. Nonetheless, vaulting over a wooden horse caused many injuries for both men and women. Men vaulted over the long horse; women cleared it turned sideways. The safety of vaults became a hot topic in the 1980s. Then when American gymnast Trent Dimas collided with the horse and landed on his head in the 1991 world championships, gymnastics equipment makers picked up the pace. In 2001 FIG eliminated the wooden horse from gymnastics competition. Both women and men gymnasts now use specially designed vaulting tables.

Jahn's students had used large wooden boards with no springs to vault. Drawings from a popular book in the 1800s, *Elements of Gym-*

nastics and of Calisthenics for Young Ladies, showed women using a springboard to vault. In the 1950s Richard Reuther invented a springboard specifically for international gymnastics competition, for many years called the Reuther board. Now it's simply called the vaulting board.

Uneven Parallel Bars

Originally gymnastics students used the parallel bars to build strength. They lifted themselves up and repeated a dipping motion many times. Modern gymnasts still use dips to increase their upper-body strength. Jahn's students discovered, however, that many swinging movements could be performed on the parallel bars.

Women gymnasts waited more than 100 years to compete on the uneven bars. In 1830 Francisco Amoros wrote about the uneven bars in a gymnastics book that became popular in France. Women began competing on the uneven bars in the 1934 world championships. But even in the 1936 Olympics, women were required to compete on the parallel bars, and only the Czechoslovakia team chose the uneven bars for the voluntary exercise. Women changed completely to the uneven bars when individual events were introduced in the 1952 Games.

Doris Fuchs Brause, an American gymnast, set new standards for the uneven bars at the world championships in Dortmund, Germany, in 1966. She performed her routine without a pause, which no woman had ever done before. Although the judge agreed that her score should have been higher, it was not changed. The crowd in Dortmund, Germany, raised a fuss and held up the competition for more than an hour. In the end Brause did not win a medal and did not even make the finals.

Floor Exercise

Before women competed in international gymnastics, they showed graceful, ballet-like moves in an exhibition at the 1912 Olympics in Stockholm, Sweden. For many years both men and women gymnasts performed floor exercises on grassy fields or bare wooden floors. The 1936 Olympics in Berlin marked the first time floor exercises were performed on a somewhat springy surface. Now gymnasts perform their routines on a much softer, carpeted surface. They lose points if they go outside the 12-meter square area (40 feet by 40 feet).

Larissa Latynina from the Soviet Union became the first star in women's gymnastics at the Melbourne Olympics in 1956. Just 21 at the time, she went on to win three consecutive Olympic gold medals in the floor exercise.

Trampoline

The trampoline became the newest gymnastics event in the 2000 Olympic Games, although its history goes back several centuries. In the 1800s circus performers bounced off devices similar to trampolines to entertain audiences. It was called a "bouncing bed" early in the next century because acrobats covered it with bedclothes to get laughs.

In the early 1930s an American gymnast named George Nissen spent four years creating a device to bounce high into the air. He and two of his college buddies showed off his invention in Mexico, where they performed as the Three Leonardos. They stayed at the Mexico City YMCA, where the local swimming and diving team worked out each day. They barely spoke Spanish, but the magical word for diving board kept coming to mind: *trampolín.* It sounded just right. When Nissen returned to the United States he added an *e* and trademarked the Trampoline.

During World War II pilots and parachutists used the trampoline to help them get used to weightlessness and different body positions in space. Astronauts also used trampolines. Trampoline training soared when Charles Pond invented a twisting belt that safely holds gymnasts while they perform somersaults in midair. In 1948 gymnasts at U.S. colleges and universities began competing in the trampoline. The first trampoline world championship was held in London in 1964.

At first Americans soared above all other international competitors. But the opportunities to compete in the United States dropped dramatically in the late 1960s when many lawsuits were brought because of trampoline injuries. Since then European countries have dominated international trampoline competition.

STAR POWER

The Soviet Union's gymnasts became the golden girls of the 1952 Helsinki Games. They swept the gold medals in all but two of the events—Hungary won the balance beam and the uneven bars. The same show went on, with the same country, but different performers, taking home most of the medals for the next 40 years. The Soviets won the team gold medal in all 10 Olympics in which they participated. (They boycotted the 1984 Los Angeles Games, and Romania won.) They reclaimed the gold medal in 1988 and won in their final appearance in the 1992 Games as the "Unified Team" after the collapse of the USSR.

Starting in 1960, the Olympics and gymnastics were shown on television. With the Soviets' gymnastics skills, almost everyone knew who would win. Still, millions of people watched the gymnastics competitions. Then in the 1972 Olympics, a tiny young Soviet gymnast named Olga Korbut charmed millions of TV viewers around the world. Her performance changed the world's view of gymnastics. Girls everywhere wanted to be like Korbut. Gymnastics schools broke new ground across the United States as enrollment went off the charts.

If Korbut brought passion to gymnastics, Nadia Comaneci of Romania proved in the 1976 Olympics that perfection was possible. Comaneci scored the first 10s in the Olympics and won the gold medal on the uneven bars, the balance beam, and the all-around competition. She made perhaps a greater impact on American gymnastics after the Olympics. Comaneci came to live in the United States, and her coach, Bela Karolyi, soon followed. Karolyi helped Mary Lou Retton become America's most famous gymnast.

In the 1984 Olympics Retton became the first American woman to win a gold medal in gymnastics. Her performance and smile lifted the gloom created by the Soviet boycott of the Los Angeles Games. Young American gymnasts now had a gold-medal role model, and once again enrollment in gymnastics schools soared.

That same year rhythmic gymnastics became part of the Olympics. This graceful type of gymnastics had debuted in competition in eastern Europe during the 1930s. In rhythmic gymnastics performers must use four of five props (a ball, a hoop, clubs, a ribbon, or a rope) in each competition. With the grace of a ballerina they move along a square floor that measures 12 meters (40 feet) on each side.

After the 1984 Olympics new stars in U.S. gymnastics emerged, such as Kim Zmeskal, Shannon Miller, Dominique Moceanu, and Kerri Strug. Despite a horribly sprained ankle, Strug's vault gave the United States team its first gold medal in the 1996 Olympics. Her bravery and stoicism created an unforgettable moment in gymnastics history.

2
GETTING STARTED

You are psyched to start a gymnastics program somewhere soon. You may want to use gymnastics to help improve in other sports. Maybe you know that gymnastics provides a solid foundation for dance, ballet, or cheerleading. Or, you may have seen top gymnasts on television and dream of being just like them. Whatever your reasons, you are convinced that gymnastics would be good for you.

In order to get started, talk about gymnastics with your parents. This means more than asking them for permission and the money to sign up for a gymnastics program. Share your thoughts about gymnastics. Your parents will ask important questions to help choose the best program for you. They will help you identify your goals and encourage you to focus on achieving them. Your parents can help make sure you get the most out of your gymnastics experience.

Decide why you want to participate in gymnastics. Are you ready to devote your time and effort to the sport? You learn gymnastics one movement at a time in a method called "progressions." First, you will be taught one move, which is called a "skill" in gymnastics. Then you master it and progress to a more challenging skill. There are no shortcuts in gymnastics, so if you miss a class, you'll have to make it up.

Beginners usually practice once a week for about one to one and a half hours. Expect to spend more time at your gym if you develop more skills and are interested in competing. Preteams and beginner teams often practice two or three times per week for one and a half to two hours per session. Classes are shorter, about 45 minutes, for preschoolers and toddlers in the "Mom and Tot" programs. Once you decide with your family that you want to make the commitment to gymnastics, you can start your search for the right place.

Your friends and family can be a great source of information about gymnastics programs in your area. Talk to your friends who are already participating in gymnastics. Ask your parents for their suggestions, too. Maybe you have older sisters or brothers who took gymnastics, and they can tell you about their experience.

Then check out the Internet, where there are hundreds of websites about gymnastics and clubs in your area. A good place to start is USA Gymnastics (www.usa-gymnastics.org), which sets the rules and policies for gymnastics in the United States. You can find the names and telephone numbers of gymnastics clubs that are members of USA Gymnastics in all of the 50 states, and there are links with a brief description of each club's programs. The United States Association of Independent Gymnastics Clubs, or USAIGC (www.usaigc.com), has information about its member clubs and different levels of competition. Your local YMCA as well as some parks and recreation departments also offer recreational gymnastics programs for beginners. The yellow pages of the phone book may provide further options. After you've gathered and reviewed all this information, you should visit the club you want to join. Most clubs will allow you and your parents to watch a lesson for free before signing up. You'll be able to meet your coaches and talk to girls who are already in the program.

SAFETY FIRST

Safety will probably be the most important factor when you and your parents choose a gymnastics program. Here's what your mom or dad should look for when you check out a club.

- Are the floors clean? There should be no loose equipment where people walk. Most gymnasts walk around barefoot, and objects on the floor could cause injuries.
- Is the building designed to reduce the risk of collisions? Are ceilings and lights high enough? All walls, doors, and windows should be a safe distance from all activities.

  Different groups may be working on developing different skills at the same time. You don't want the possibility of someone jumping into an area where other girls are practicing tumbling. That's why it's a good idea for activities to be arranged by stations. There should be an assigned area to practice each skill. There should be enough space between the apparatus to eliminate the risk of collisions.
- Is the equipment placed away from sunlight that might shine in a gymnast's eyes? Such a distraction can cause injury.

- How often are the equipment and mats inspected and maintained? The equipment should be adjustable for different ages.
- Is the trampoline built into the floor? That's a huge safety advantage. Built-in trampolines reduce the risk of injuries because the springs are not placed around the edges of the trampoline. But on standard trampolines, many injuries occur when the child bounces off the edge and lands on a wooden floor or crashes into a wall. Children who get on regular trampolines constantly have to be reminded to stay in the center and avoid the risk of being bounced off.

CHOOSING YOUR CLUB

Your parents probably have some important questions about the club. Does the club have a mission statement, or operating philosophy? How can beginners benefit by signing up for the program? Most gymnastics clubs have a brochure that you and your parents should read. Most likely the brochure will describe the teaching approach and objectives for different age groups. Some clubs have a lesson plan that describes what you will learn each week. Your parents may want to see this step-by-step guide because it shows how the club will help you achieve your goals.

The club's brochure will also give you the basics. You need to know class schedules, the length of the sessions, and the cost of the program. How long has the school been in business? Does it belong to gymnastics organizations such as USA Gymnastics and USAIGC? What is its sales pitch? Is safety emphasized?

Gymnastics clubs usually organize classes for beginners by age. Does the club offer sessions for girls in your age group? Will you be in a class with girls who have similar physical abilities? Will everyone in your group start with the same level of gymnastics experience?

How far is the club from home? How are you going to get there?

You should choose a program that matches your interest and commitment to gymnastics. Before you sign up, ask to observe a class in your age group. If the school lets you look in on a class—and it should—take advantage of the opportunity. While you're there, take into consideration the following:

- Instructors are responsible for supervising the safety of participants who perform a skill (or a series of skills) on the apparatus. This is called "spotting," and it's one of the most important parts of an instructor's job.

- Do the students pay attention when the instructor is demonstrating a new skill? If not, does the instructor redo the skill so that everybody clearly sees how it is to be done?
- Do the instructors show patience with less talented athletes? Do they offer encouragement? Are the instructors enthusiastic? And the participants?
- How many students are assigned to each instructor? For children who are five and older, the ratio should be a maximum of 10 to one, but USA Gymnastics recommends eight students per instructor. For preschool programs (ages two to five), USA Gymnastics suggests that the ratio should not be higher than six to one.
- As your parents watch, they will also have an opportunity to talk to other parents. How do the parents of participants measure their children's progress since they started the program? How do the parents compare their expectations to the children's actual performance? How do their children like the program? Do the children talk about it often, and what do they say?
- Watch the girls' expressions after they perform a skill and wait for their next turn. Are they smiling? Do they seem to be enjoying the lesson? Talk to them after they finish their lesson. Ask them if they're having fun. Does the instructor clearly explain and show them how to do different skills? Do they feel that they're learning and progressing?

Many gymnastics programs refer to themselves as schools or academies for good reason. When you enroll in a gymnastics program, you are learning a whole new set of skills. So your coach is really a teacher. Your parents should ask about your coach's credentials. Where did he or she study? What awards or competitions has he or she won?

USA Gymnastics offers a safety certification course for gymnastics instructors, as well as a two-level Professional Development Program. Has your instructor completed either, or both, of these programs? In its effort to promote continuing education for its instructors, USA Gymnastics also offers seminars, clinics, and workshops. Does your instructor attend these seminars and workshops?

How many years has the instructor taught your age group? Someone who has coached elite teenage gymnasts for five years certainly has the knowledge but may not have ever taught beginners.

It's a good idea for you and your parents to meet your coach or instructor before you sign up. Talk to the coach, and you will get an idea of his or her personality. Is the person warm, positive, caring, funny? Why does he or she like teaching gymnastics?

ACCIDENTS CAN HAPPEN

Regardless of the instructor's qualifications, accidents will sometimes happen in gymnastics. Is your instructor trained in first aid and CPR? Does the school have planned procedures to respond to a serious injury? In such cases, quick and effective treatment is extremely important.

What happens if you get hurt? What are the school's policies when an injury occurs? Is insurance included when you enroll in the class? Or do you have to pay a separate fee for registration and insurance?

While you wait for all the paperwork to be done, many exciting thoughts may be rushing through your mind. There's a lot happening on the floor, too. It is hard to focus on one activity because six different skills are being practiced at the same time. A group of girls waits by the balance beam while one works to find her footing. At another station, with a blue and yellow mat that looks like a cheese wedge, a girl, helped by her instructor, does her first backward roll. Several feet away, girls run about 20 yards before they jump off a springboard onto a two-foot-high heavily padded mat. Another group of girls wait their turn at the uneven bars. Others wait their turn while each girl gets to jump on the trampoline. In the far corner, a girl who climbs the rope up to the height of her instructor proudly smiles.

You will see different types of mats underneath all the gymnastics apparatus; in fact, mats should cover the entire area of gymnastics activity. Mats are a sort of security blanket, because they soften the impact of landing and reduce the risk of injuries, although they do not offer 100 percent protection.

The standard floor mats are about two inches thick. When you step on them, they bounce back instantly to their original shape because they are made of hard material. The landing mats used in gymnastics competition are four inches thick and are placed underneath the balance beam, uneven bars, and vault. You will have a thicker safety cushion when you learn new skills. Your gymnastics center will add mats that are either eight inches or 12 inches thick to provide extra protection. These mats are also much wider and longer than the competitive mats underneath. Here's a quick description of the gymnastics apparatus where you will develop your skills.

- **Tumbling area:** This is a carpeted area where advanced gymnasts perform a carefully planned series of jumps, flips, twists, and turns. Beginners warm up and stretch here. You will learn all of your basic skills here or on a separate section of mats. You will need to learn how to do basic tumbling before you can progress to other gymnastics events.

- **Balance beam:** You will probably see at least three or four beams that are adjusted to different heights. The balance beam used in competitive gymnastics stands about four feet high and is 16 feet long. You will start on a balance beam that is raised only about six inches above the floor. The beam is only four inches wide, so learning how to walk will be a new and challenging experience. When you find your footing and feel comfortable, you will practice tumbling on the beam. If you learn to tumble well on the floor, your skills will transfer to the beam easily. As you raise the level of your skills, you will practice on higher and higher balance beams.
- **Uneven bars:** This gymnastics event is very different from the others. Here you have to learn to support yourself with your hands by holding onto the bar when you're hanging under it or by pushing off the bar when you're above it. Tumbling skills are important on the uneven bars, particularly on the dismount, when you have to learn to land with your knees bent.
- **Vaulting:** You use a springboard and vaulting table to launch yourself high into the air. Most beginners start jumping onto low, soft mats instead of the vaulting table to make it more fun and safe. Eventually, you will progress and run full speed toward a vaulting table that's almost as tall as you are. Your goal will be to do a tumbling trick over the vaulting table.
- **Mini-trampoline:** This gives you much more spring than an ordinary springboard, so you have to be extra careful. The "mini-tramp" makes it easier to learn how to do special skills, but it is also more dangerous because of its extra spring.
- **Trampoline:** Trampoline is a competitive event, but for beginning gymnasts it offers a safe way to practice moves and get used to the feeling of controlling their bodies in midair.
- **Climbing rope:** This is not really a gymnastics event, but using it can develop upper-body strength, which is very important. Never climb a rope without a spotter or a mat underneath you. You don't have to climb very high to get upper-body strength, just often.
- **Obstacle courses:** Toddlers in the Moms and Tots program and preschoolers love to crawl and climb. Many facilities set up equipment so that they can have fun and develop motor skills.

A COMFORTABLE FIT

You've found the right club and registered. Tomorrow's your first day. You're ready to roll, except for one thing. What do you wear?

Think comfortable and simple. Pick your favorite shorts and T-shirt. A leotard is fine, too. Your club may have leotards or special outfits that you like. Once you make progress, maybe you'll be able to buy something to show that you're a proud and successful student.

You don't have to worry about shoes, but buy several pairs of non-slip ankle socks. You'll get a better grip with your feet, especially when you're on the balance beam.

Always try to reduce the risk of injuries; gymnastics is challenging enough. Don't wear jewelry, which most clubs won't allow anyway. If you have long hair, tie it back securely to prevent it from getting caught in the equipment. Do not use sharp hairpins, which could break off and cause serious injury. Do not put your hair in braids, which can catch on equipment.

YOUR FIRST DAY

You've done all this reading and research about gymnastics, but still you feel a little bit scared about your first day. It's normal to feel nervous. The butterflies will go away.

Remember, the girls in your group will be your age, and you will all be starting something brand new. All the other girls in your group don't really know what practice is going to be like, either. In fact, you have an advantage: You have read about gymnastics and know what to expect.

You will learn gymnastics one small move at a time. It's like putting together a puzzle. You do a lot of work, spend a lot of time, and then everything comes together. The same will happen with gymnastics. Be patient. Just ask your gymnastics instructor. She or he has taught many girls like you and knows how to help you feel comfortable. So, take a deep breath and relax. Feeling comfortable and confident will help you make the right moves in gymnastics. Your instructor will show and tell you what to do and will be your biggest booster. Above all, get ready to have fun.

3
The Safe Approach

Soon you will stand tall on a balance beam, race down a runway, and jump from a springboard to fly through the air, swing freely, and turn upside down on the high bar. But before you get off the ground in gymnastics, you need to learn how to stay safe.

You need to know the risks. The gymnastics apparatus stands above the floor, so much of the time you will perform skills in the air. Sometimes you will turn upside down.

Landing carefully is extremely important, as a poorly placed dismount or fall can cause head, neck, or back injuries or, at worst, permanent paralysis. It's important to understand that the jumps, flips, and twists and turns performed high in the air create a lot of energy that is absorbed when you land.

Now you see why it is so important to learn how to land and fall safely; in fact, the USA Gymnastics safety manual recommends that the first thing you should learn is how to fall. There is always a risk of physical injury in gymnastics, but there are proven ways to reduce the risk. First and most important, safety is an attitude for you and your gymnastics club.

The best gymnastics clubs emphasize safety from the moment you walk in until you leave. They start you off slowly. Your instructor will supervise every move you make. If you had any thoughts—or worries—about walking on a high balance beam the first few days, forget them. Remember, you learn the simplest skills in a step-by-step method called progressions. First, you build the basics on the ground so that you have a solid foundation, then you progress higher up to the apparatus.

SPOTTING

The first time you try a skill, your instructor will spot you to make sure you are safe. Your instructor has spotted girls just like you hundreds of times. That should put your mind at ease.

Proper spotting provides a safety net for gymnasts. But that doesn't mean that every move you make in gymnastics class needs to be spotted. For example, with your instructor's permission, you will practice certain tumbling skills and walk on a low balance beam by yourself. The purpose of spotting is to give you the self-confidence and security to perform a move by yourself.

If you rely too heavily on the spotter, it will take much longer to learn the skill. It's a good sign when your spotter pulls back and lets you perform. Eventually you will be able to do many skills by yourself. Your instructor knows how to provide just the right touch of spotting to let you develop your skills.

The USA Gymnastics Safety Manual describes the purposes of spotting as follows:

- To demonstrate proper body positions throughout a skill.
- To identify the important changes of body position or transitions throughout a skill.
- To give the athlete verbal or physical cues, such as a light touch.
- To physically assist the entire skill or part of a skill when necessary.
- To encourage participants to build their confidence and help eliminate their fear.
- To assist the completion of a skill to ensure the athlete's safety.

You will make your spotter's job easier by following these few simple rules.

- Tell your spotter what you're doing before you start. Are you doing a front somersault or back somersault? Which direction are you going to dismount off the high bar?
- Make sure the instructor is ready to spot you.
- Let the spotter know if this is the first time you've performed the skill. If you have done a skill before, you will be spotted differently.
- Be prepared for occasional contact. Your instructor might accidentally touch you where it normally would be socially unacceptable (such as the buttocks or chest). Or, you might accidentally hit your instructor in a similar "no zone." In either case, "Oops," or "Sorry about that," is the proper response.

MATS

When you start practicing on the apparatus, there will be piles of mats everywhere underneath you. Every possible landing area will be covered. That's because gymnastics clubs give beginners a wider margin of error. The extra layers of soft landing mats will give you more protection and peace of mind. Beginners have a wider margin of error. You will also use more mats when you start learning more difficult skills. Keep in mind that the mats can only soften the impact of a landing. They are only one factor in the formula for safety.

HELP YOURSELF

You control what happens while you're in the air. You will learn how to protect yourself if you fall. Of course, you play the biggest part in your own safety. The following are some things you can do to help stay safe.

- Learn and obey the rules of your gymnastics club. For example, there are certain places where you should never walk, especially in front of someone else's possible landing area. If you're not sure about something, always ask.
- Always check the mats before you start a skill. When other gymnasts practice, the mats can move, which creates a gap. If you see a gap in the matting, immediately point this out to your instructor. Don't start your move until your instructor or someone else fixes the matting.
- Make sure you get permission from your instructor to work on a skill. You might walk on a low balance beam while others in your group try a higher beam with your instructor. For your safety, your instructor should know what you're doing at all times.
- Always ask if you have questions about a skill. Gymnastics offers enough challenges even when you know exactly what you're supposed to do. Clear up any questions before you take your turn.
- Stay within your limits. If you're not sure that you can do something, ask your instructor if you are ready to try the skill. Remember to be patient. There are plenty of other skills to practice.
- Keep your eyes open at all times when you are performing a skill. There is a fear factor in gymnastics, and it tends to make some girls close their eyes. This is not a good idea, as you lose your body awareness, which means knowing where you are in

relation to the ground and the apparatus. When you shut your eyes, you also lose your balance. (Normally your eyes and brain exchange information about balance. With your eyes shut, the balance signals become disconnected.) When you can't use your senses, the risk of injury rises dramatically. Keep your eyes open.
- Complete each skill. When you start a skill, complete the movement and follow through.

LEARNING TO FALL

Falling is part of gymnastics. For safety's sake it is the first thing you should learn. You can prevent injuries by knowing how to fall properly. You should learn how to fall forward, backward, and sideways.

Most of the time falling is sudden and unexpected. You want to learn how to use the correct falling skills automatically. Your goal is to spread the force of the landing across the greatest possible distance, time, and area of your body. Short, quick impacts to a specific area of the body are the most likely to cause injury. You can practice these progressions to improve your falling skills.

FORWARD FALLING

Start in a push-up position on your knees, on a soft landing mat either four inches or eight inches thick. Land on your hands and chest to provide support for the rest of your body. Turn your head to the side to protect your face.

Now, as a variation, start in a push-up position. Bend your elbows as you fall forward to the floor. Turn your head to the side and land on your chest. Break the fall with your bent arms.

Next, kneel with your arms at your sides, and repeat the previous drill.

Start from a standing position and drop to your knees. Repeat Step 3 several times. As you learn how to control your fall, practice hitting the ground faster and harder.

Finally, stand on a raised surface, such as a folded panel mat. Fall from the standing position onto the soft mat. Absorb the impact with bent arms and landing on your thighs and chest to distribute the impact of the fall safely.

BACKWARD FALLING

Lie on your back on a soft landing mat. Round your back and shoulders. Bend your knees and bring them up to your chin on your chest.

Rock back and forth to get the feel of a rounded back while you're moving. Keep your chin on your chest by tightening your neck and shoulder muscles just enough. Keep your protected round shape to avoid whiplash. Put your palms and forearms on the mat (thumbs in toward your body, fingers pointed toward your toes) to absorb the impact of more powerful falls later on.

Next, bend your knees and squat down. Fall backward while holding the same rounded position described in Step 1. Keep your chin on your chest. Repeat this drill with more and more force.

Stand and drop to a squatting position. Fall back to the rounded body position described in Step 1.

SIDEWAYS FALLING

Kneel down. Fall forward while turning sideways. Roll over using your shoulder.

Stand, then drop to your knees while turning sideways slightly. Fall first with your thigh, then your hip and shoulder to make contact with the floor.

THINK SMALL

You have seen top gymnasts perform with amazing grace and beauty. They put their skills on display in spectacular combinations. Up until now it may have been hard for you to tell when one skill stops and the next one starts. You're about to find out that gymnasts at every level break each skill into many small motions. They practice every seemingly simple movement, such as holding your legs straight in front of you, hundreds of times.

You will follow the same formula to be successful in gymnastics: You have to think small before you look at the big picture. Consider each gymnastics skill part of a puzzle. You learn how to put your body in the right position to perform a skill. One skill leads to the next. Then you work on combinations of skills.

Say you want to do a cartwheel, one of the most popular skills in gymnastics. You have to be able to do a handstand to kick your legs straight above you. You must also learn how to land safely on your feet. All of your repetitions and conditioning exercises will pay off. Be patient. You will make progress and soon you will do cartwheels that will make your friends say, "Wow."

Gymnastics is very different from most other sports, such as soccer. Surely you have seen or heard about someone who suddenly kicks a spectacular goal. This can be a one-time event, a lucky shot. Yet such success quickly disappears if the athlete can't regularly perform the basics.

Success won't come suddenly in gymnastics. You will have to earn it. The rewards of performing a skill may well take many hours of practice. At first you will not be familiar with the skills. You may need to develop the strength and flexibility of certain muscles to perform some skills. Of course, you must set your goals and follow a plan to achieve them. Gymnastics will always test your mind and your will to succeed.

For instance, what happens if you try a gymnastics trick many times without good results? You need courage to go to your coach and ask for help, self-discipline to stick to your coach's suggestions, determination to do it the new way, and patience to keep practicing until you get it right. Eventually all this effort will pay off. You will get to show everyone what you learned. You will increase your self-confidence. Gymnastics will make you physically and mentally stronger. You will learn how to face and conquer your fears. That's why so many girls find gymnastics challenging and rewarding.

LEARNING YOUR LESSONS

Your success in gymnastics will depend on what you do during your lessons. It's very important to listen to your instructor and watch carefully when she or he shows your group how to do a skill.

When you're at home, you can do flexibility, balance, and strength exercises to help improve your skills. But your gymnastics club is the place where you will make progress, so your time in the gym is precious. Here are some golden rules to make the most of your time.

- Watch, listen, and wait for your turn. It's OK to have a good time with your classmates, but watch and listen when the instructor shows your group how to do a skill. You can also learn by watching the girls in your group take their turns. Pay attention and always be ready. Your turn may be next.
- Stay with your group. Classes move quickly. There are many skills to learn. During a typical lesson, you'll spend about 15 minutes on each set of skills before your group moves to a different station. Be prepared to move quickly and follow your group.
- Be ready to learn. You will be introduced to new skills or something slightly different each day. Ask questions if you don't understand something. If you're not sure, ask your instructor to show you the skill again. Remember, you have to know what to do before you can do it.

- Get ready for a lot of repetitions. At each station, you will review the skills you have already learned in previous lessons. You have to master the basics first, therefore, you need the repetitions.
- At the end of each event, you might have a contest. Have fun with it. Maybe you'll perform the best handstand or have the highest or longest jump from the vaulting board. If you don't win, don't worry. One of the joys of gymnastics is that you can always do better the next time. Remember that you can compete against yourself (and others), have fun, and develop skills at the same time.
- Learn the language of gymnastics. Like most sports, gymnastics has its own language. For instance, you do a forward roll on the floor, but you do a forward somersault in midair. A somersault is also called a "flip" or "salto."

  Your coach will explain all the terms, and the glossary at the end of the book will help you remember them. When you learn the lingo, your coach can spend more time on coaching, and you can spend more time practicing your skills. Plus, you will be able to tell your friends and family everything you've learned.

BUILDING YOUR FOUNDATION

Tumbling is your ticket to success in gymnastics. You enter the floor exercise area and start practicing the forward roll, handstand, and many other building-block skills. These will be your foundation in gymnastics. You will use them to progress to the balance beam, vault, and uneven bars. In fact, the forward roll on the floor and the balance beam are nearly the same, except you have only a four-inch landing area on the beam. That's a very thin margin of error. The adjustable height of the beam raises the challenge of the forward roll to another level.

Similarly, you perform a handstand the same way on the floor as you do on the vault, uneven bars, and the balance beam. But when you take a running start and launch yourself head over heels to clear the vault, it is much more challenging than a handstand on the floor.

Of course, you need to learn the basic skills first. It will take time for you to feel comfortable and confident with the basics. No one gets them right the first time, or even the 10th. Your instructor might use many teaching tools to help you get started. For example, you might use the high end of a mat shaped like a cheese wedge when you first practice the backward roll. It's a lot easier to roll downhill, but be prepared. You will roll faster and that could be scary. As you improve, your instructor will make the angle of the mats less steep. Eventually you will be able to do the backward roll on a flat surface.

You may find some skills difficult to learn. Ask your coach for help. She can give you some tips that help you make progress. Always remember—some skills may take more time to learn than others.

Gymnastics requires repetitions, and you will get plenty of chances to practice these skills. Your confidence will grow and strength improve with practice. Meanwhile your instructor will show you new moves. With practice and patience you will be able to perform a basic skill, such as the forward roll, without even thinking about it. Your instructor will let you know when your skills are solid. When you get the green light, you will move to the next skill in the progression.

Eventually, you will be ready to put two or more moves together, known as a combination. The quality of your combinations will depend on your ability to perform the basic skills. That's why even the top gymnasts in the world always practice the basics. And you will, too.

4 CONDITIONING

By now you've thought a lot about gymnastics. You've talked about it with your friends and family, learned as much as you can, and carefully chosen your school. You are mentally ready for gymnastics.

The next step is to get your body ready. You need flexibility to move into the proper positions and have the strength to hold those positions. Conditioning prepares your body for gymnastics. Think of conditioning as a blueprint for your body. Without this plan your body wouldn't know what to do next.

Preparing your body for gymnastics is made up of four steps: warm-up, stretching, strengthening, and cooldown. You can do many of these exercises at home or at the gym. All are important for you to do as they will help you avoid injury and make it easier for you to progress to higher levels of gymnastics.

Follow these exercises regularly and gymnastics will become easier. Remember, your conditioning program is designed to help you perform your gymnastics skills. Part of becoming a gymnast involves placing unfamiliar demands and stresses on your body. Conditioning gives you the best chance to meet those demands and stay healthy.

WARM-UP

Before you put your muscles to work, they need a gentle wake-up call. All sorts of alarms in your body help your muscles start moving. Your body temperature rises and your muscles get warm. That's why it's called a "warm-up." Your heart starts pumping faster so that fresh blood circulates through your body and brings oxygen to

TOP 10 REASONS TO WARM UP AND STRETCH

10. First-rate gymnasts warm up, so you should too.
9. You'll always be warm during workouts.
8. You'll feel proud when your face changes color.
7. It gives you time to get ready for the new lesson.
6. It relaxes your entire body and mind.
5. You can make new friends with your stretching partner.
4. When you try to do a split, your body will say thank you.
3. It gives you more energy.
2. It reduces the risk of injuries.
1. It feels great!

your muscles. Your muscles then loosen up so it's easier to stretch them out.

What happens when you don't warm up? It's sort of like taking a shower without hot water or when someone wakes you up unexpectedly. Without warm-up, if you move quickly, you could strain a muscle or damage a bone, because your muscles are suddenly working without proper notice. These injuries can be very painful and can keep you out of gymnastics for quite a while.

Many of these problems can be prevented by spending the time and effort to warm up properly every time. Think of warming up as an investment in your body: It reduces the risk of injuries.

There are many ways to warm up. Start slowly with each exercise and then pick up the pace. Different exercises make your warm-up more interesting. It really doesn't matter how you get your muscles moving, as long as you get the blood circulating. Any combination of the following exercises will work fine.

- Walk around a circle, then jog slowly. Go three or four times around the circle. Jog the other way around the circle. Jog backward.
- Jog sideways in a gallop once around. Gallop in the other direction.
- Spread your feet about shoulder-width. Slide one foot next to the other and repeat this dance movement, which is called a "chassé." Repeat in the opposite direction.
- Hop on one foot at least three times. Repeat with the other foot.
- Skip forward once around the circle. Skip backward for at least a few steps.
- Jump around the circle with both feet together.

- Spin around and return to your original position. Repeat several times.
- Do some jumping jacks. Start with your feet together. Put your arms at the sides. Jump and spread your feet apart while you swing your arms over your head. Return to the original position.

STRETCHING

Once you have warmed up your muscles, you are ready to perform stretching exercises. These exercises should take up no more than about 10 or 15 minutes and will prepare your body for the demands you are about to place on it.

The purpose of stretching is to loosen tight muscles and relax your body. These exercises are supposed to feel good. You should never feel pain while stretching.

Stretch slowly and smoothly. Continue until you feel a full stretch. Your body will let you know how far to stretch. Stop before it hurts. Hold each stretch for at least five seconds. Do not bounce or force your body to stretch beyond its natural limit. That increases the risk of tearing a muscle. Remember, stretching is supposed to prevent injuries, not cause them.

There are hundreds of stretching exercises. Your instructor will decide which ones are the best for you and your class. Following are some basic stretches used by gymnasts.

Hamstring

Sit on the floor with your feet flexed against a wall. Keeping your back flat, lean forward with your arms extended at shoulder height until you can touch the wall with your fists. Return to the starting position.

Short Split Forward

Kneel with your back straight, one leg bent, and the other stretched straight out in front of you. Keeping your back flat and your front leg straight, lower your chest to about a 45-degree angle. Next, bend your front knee forward, keeping your foot in front of your knee and your shoulders in line with your hips. Press your hips toward the floor so that you are doing a split of about 120 degrees.

Straddle Split

Lie on your back with your buttocks against a wall. Raise your legs vertically and separate them, keeping them fully extended, until they

Short split forward (above and below)

form a 90-degree angle. Hold and slowly return both legs to a vertical position.

Shoulder Flexibility

Lie on your stomach on the floor with your arms stretched overhead in front of you and your chin touching the floor. Hold a wooden dowel or other light bar with your palms pointed down and wrists straight. Holding the bar with your hands together so your thumbs are touching,

Straddle split (above)

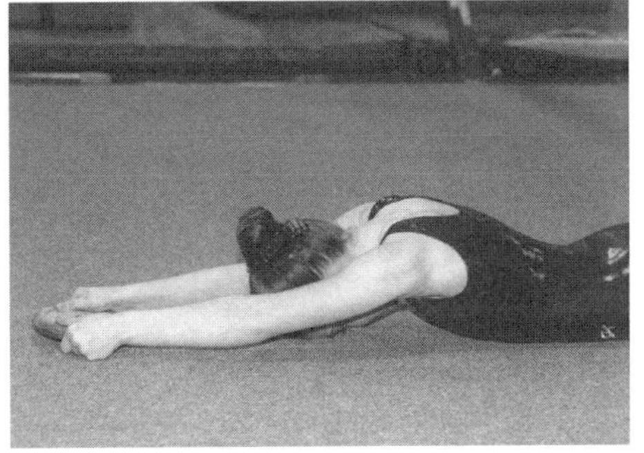

Shoulder flexibility (above and right)

slowly raise the bar a minimum of four inches above the floor. Keep your arms straight and your chin on the floor during this exercise.

Back Flexibility

Lie on your back with your knees bent and your feet flat on the floor about shoulder-width apart. Put your hands on the mat, palms down and pointing toward your feet. Push against the floor and arch your back into a bridge position, extending your legs and straightening your arms. Hold. Return to the starting position.

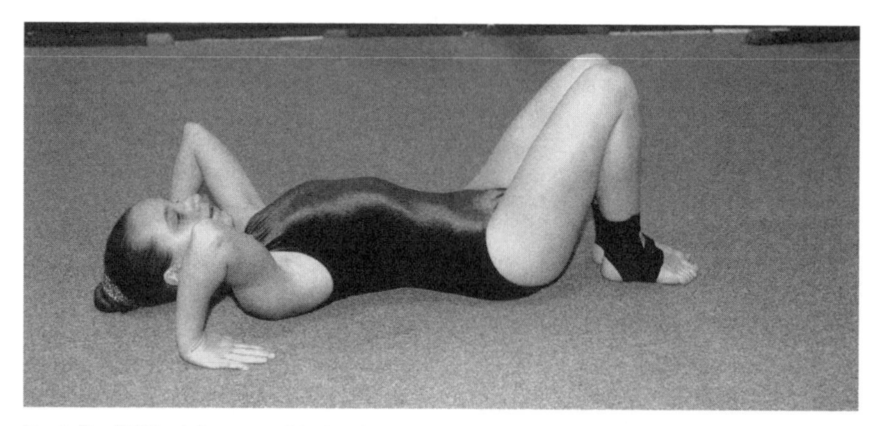

Back flexibility (above and below)

HEAD AND NECK

Here are some other stretches you may want to try. Be sure to proceed gradually, and ask your coach or instructor for advice on the best stretches for you.

Chin Circles

Reach your chin forward. With your chin, draw a circle down and around, ending with your chin tucked back toward your throat. Repeat five times. Reverse the direction of the circle, and repeat five times.

Head Lift

Lie down, bend your knees, lift your head, and lace your fingers behind your head. Use your arms to pull your head forward slowly. You should feel the stretch in the back of your neck. Hold the stretch for a count of five. Slowly return to the starting position. Repeat five times.

Head Rotation to the Side

Slowly turn your head to one side. Hold the stretch for a count of three. Slowly return to the starting position. Then turn your head to the other side. Hold the stretch for a count of three. Return to the starting position. Repeat five to 10 times. Try doing a set two or three times a day.

ARMS, SHOULDERS, AND WRISTS

Arm Circles

Standing, grasp a chair with one arm. Bend forward at the waist. To protect your back, you should bend your knees a bit. The free arm should hang down; your shoulder blade should be down. Swing your arm in small circles. Repeat motion and change direction of circles.

Arm Stretch

With your right hand, grasp your left elbow in front of you. Look over your left shoulder, and pull your left elbow toward your right shoulder. Hold for 15 counts. Repeat two or three times. Do the other side.

Flexing Wrists

With your fingers extended, flex your wrist and stretch your fingers up to the ceiling and down to the floor. Repeat 10 to 20 times. Do the same for the other wrist.

Raised Arms 1

Stand straight and raise your arms straight above your head. Rise up on your toes and clench your fists. Hold for 10 to 15 seconds. In this position, spread your fingers apart. Rotate your hands in one direction five times, then in the other direction five times.

Raised Arms 2

Stand straight and your raise arms straight above your head. Lace your fingers together, palms facing up. Push your arms back and up, until you feel the stretch in your arms, shoulders, and back. Hold for 10 to 15 seconds. Repeat four to six times.

Rotating Wrists

Make a fist, and rotate your hand from the wrist. Do this in one direction 10 times, and in the other direction 10 times. Next, open your fist, and rotate your hand with the fingers extended. Repeat on the other side.

Shoulder Blade Crunch

Interlace your fingers behind your head. Move your elbows back to pinch your shoulder blades together. Hold for three counts and relax. Repeat three times.

Shoulder Blade Stretch

While standing or sitting, reach around your chest and try to grasp your shoulder blades with your opposite hands. Drop your chin toward your chest. Inhale and hold onto your shoulder blades for a count of 15. You should feel the stretch along the border of your shoulder blades.

BACK AND CHEST

Back and Arms Stretch

Standing, link your hands together behind your back. Rotate your elbows inward while you straighten your arms.

Back and Chest Stretch

Standing, link your hands together behind your back. Lift your arms up until you feel a nice stretch. Hold for 10 to 20 seconds. Repeat as you like.

Bending Side to Side

Stand with your arms by your sides. Bend from the waist toward one side and then the other. Repeat up to 50 times.

The Cat

On the floor get on your hands and knees. Start with your back flat; keep your arms straight. Let your lower back sink as far as possible, without raising your head, to a concave position. After, slowly arch your back until you're curled in a convex position. Repeat 15 to 20 times.

Lower Back Stretch

Lie on the floor and relax your back muscles. Slowly bring your knees up to your chest. Curl your arms around your knees. Hold for 15 to 20 seconds. Repeat 10 times. You can also do this exercise with one leg at a time.

LEGS

Quadriceps Stretch 1

Lie on your side, resting the side of your head in your hand. Stretch your bottom leg straight on the floor. Bend your top leg, hold the foot, and pull the heel toward the buttock. Hold for 10 to 20 seconds. Repeat four to five times.

Quadriceps Stretch 2

Sit with one leg bent, touching the heel of the foot to the buttock. You can bend the other leg as well or leave it straight in front of you. Hold for 10 to 20 seconds. Repeat four to five times.

KNEES, ANKLES, AND FEET

Achilles Tendon Stretch

Stand arm's length from a wall and lean forward on your hands against the wall. Move one foot forward and one foot back a bit. Keep the heel of the back foot flat on the floor. Stretch forward until you feel the stretch in the back of the knee of the back leg. Hold for 10 seconds. Unlock the back knee and bend it toward the wall until you feel the stretch in the lower leg, closer to the heel. Hold for 10 seconds. Repeat eight to 10 times. Switch legs.

Ankle and Calf Stretch

Sit back in a chair with your feet flat on the floor. Keeping your heels on the floor, lean forward in the chair. If necessary, push your knees down. Hold for 45 seconds. Repeat five to 10 times.

Ankle Circles

Sit on the floor or in a chair. Remove shoes and socks. Moving only the ankle of one foot, draw circles. Repeat 10 to 20 times. Switch to the other ankle.

Drawing the Alphabet

Sit on the floor or in a chair. Remove shoes and socks. Moving only the ankle of one foot, draw the letter *A* on the floor. Do the entire alphabet once, alternating feet.

CONDITIONING

The following exercises are designed to prepare your muscles for the stresses they will have to bear during routine gymnastics movements. You may have to demonstrate that you can perform each of these conditioning exercises the required number of times before you can move up to the next level and start learning more demanding routines.

Rope Climb

Stand at the base of a rope and climb hand over hand until you can touch a mark 12 feet up on the rope. You can use your legs to help you or just use your arms. Pause when you get to 12 feet and slowly come down using the same method you used to climb up.

Once you have mastered this exercise, try starting from a sitting position on the floor and climb up to the 12-foot mark. As you get stronger, start from a sitting position and climb to the 12-foot mark, pause, climb back down, touch your feet to the floor, and immediately climb back up to the six-foot mark. Pause and climb back down.

Rope climb

Pull-ups

Hang (without swinging) on the high bar using an overgrip. Keeping your legs extended and back straight, pull yourself up until your chin is above the bar. Without swinging, lower yourself back down. As you get stronger, do two pull-ups, then three, then four.

Pull-ups (above and both below)

Leg Lifts

Hang (without swinging) on the high bar and lift your legs upward, keeping them closed and fully extended, until your toes touch the bar. Lower your legs downward until you are in a long hang. Start out doing five leg lifts, then progress to eight, then 10.

Thirty-Second Hollow-Body Hold

Lie on your back with your hands extended over your head. Put your hands on top of your thighs and slide them down toward your knees as you raise your legs off the floor, bending your knees slightly. Lift your shoulders off the ground so your back is rounded. Your back and shoulders should be about six inches off the ground, while your lower back should remain on the floor. Hold for 30 seconds. Repeat four more times. Progress to sets of eight, then 10.

Leg lifts (left and both below)

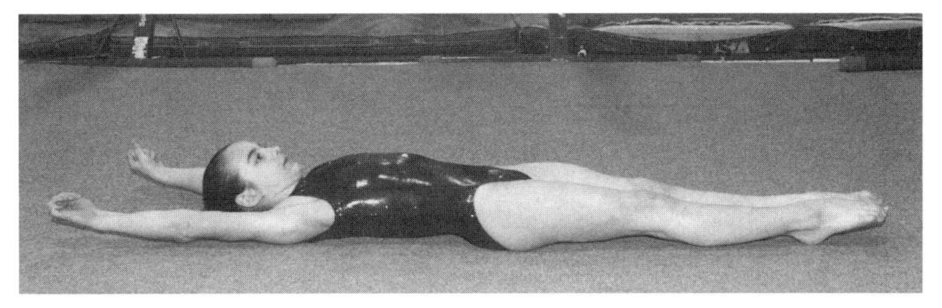

Hollow-body hold (above and below)

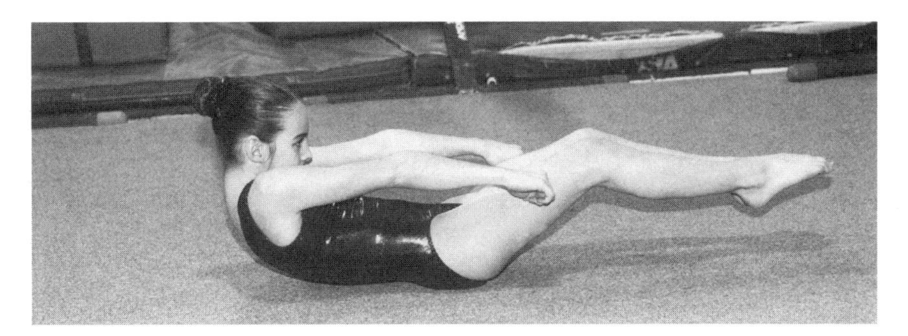

Push-ups

From a standard push-up starting position—legs and arms extended, body at a 30-degree angle to the floor—bend your arms (keeping your elbows close to your sides) and lower your body until it is two inches off the floor. Push your body back up to the starting position by straightening your arms. Begin with as many as you are able to do, the goal being to do 10 push-ups comfortably.

Push-ups (above and top of next page)

Candlestick to Straight Jumps

From a standing position with your arms fully extended over your head, bend your knees into a tuck sit position, and roll backward into a candlestick position—legs pointing straight upward with your body supported by your neck and shoulders. Roll forward to a tuck stand

Candlestick to straight jump (above and top of next page)

and, in one motion, do a straight jump upward. Repeat this exercise six times to start, then gradually increase to nine, then 12, then 15.

NECK, SHOULDERS, AND BACK

Here are some other strengthening exercises you may want to try. Be sure to proceed gradually, and ask your coach or instructor for advice on the best stretches for you.

Abdominal Crunch 1

Lie on the floor, with your knees bent. Cross your arms on your chest, and use your stomach muscles to curl your head and shoulders toward your thighs. Hold for only a few seconds. Repeat 15 to 20 times.

Abdominal Crunch 2

Lie on the floor, with your knees bent. Place your hands under your hips, and use your stomach muscles to bring one knee up to your chest. Hold for five to 10 seconds. Repeat 10 to 20 times.

Buttock Muscle Stretch

On the floor get on your hands and knees. Keep your eyes facing the floor. Lift one leg and stretch it out, parallel to the floor. Hold for five to 10 seconds. Repeat four to six times. Switch to the other leg.

Pelvic Tilt

Lie on the floor, with your knees bent. Slowly tighten your stomach and buttock muscles as you press your lower back to the floor. Hold for 10 seconds. Repeat five to 10 times. You can also lift your pelvis a bit while you are tightening your stomach and buttocks, slowly rolling from your hipbone to your lower back.

Shoulder and Upper Back Exercise

On the floor get on your hands and knees. Keep your eyes facing the floor. Stretch one arm out, parallel to the floor. Hold for five to 10 seconds. Repeat four to six times. Switch to the other arm.

LEGS AND KNEES

Abductor Raise

Lie on your side, propped on one elbow. The leg on the floor is bent. The other leg is straight. Slowly, lift the leg, hold it up for five seconds, lower it. (Using ankle weights increases the effectiveness.) Repeat 20 to 30 times. Switch to the other side.

Assisted Knee Extension

Lie on a flat, firm surface. Keep one leg straight and bend the other. Place a small bolster, such as a rolled-up towel, under the ankle of the straight leg. Push down from the bottom of the thigh of the straight leg, thereby contracting your quadriceps muscles. Extend the knee just as much as it takes to straighten the leg, being careful to not hyperextend. Hold for a count of six. Do three sets of 10. Repeat exercise with the other leg.

Hamstring Curl

Stand with your thighs against a surface, such as facing a table or a wall. Bend one knee, as far as it can go, and hold for 10 seconds. Lower the foot slowly. (Using ankle weights increases the effectiveness.) Repeat 20 to 30 times. Switch to the other leg.

Hamstring to Deep Lunge

Kneeling, place one leg straight in front and bend at waist extending hands alongside the leg, then beyond the extended foot. This stretches the hamstring muscles of the extended leg. Lift up slowly to a kneeling position, with the spine vertical to floor and the leg still extended. Bend the extended leg at the knee and lean your chest over it, placing your hands alongside the foot of the extended leg. Extend the opposite leg to the rear and slowly stretch. Repeat on other side.

Heel Slide

Lie on a flat, firm surface. Gently slide one leg toward your chest while keeping your heel on the floor. Bend your knee as much as you can, as long as there is no pain. If you are in pain, do not bend more than 90 degrees. Straighten the leg by sliding your heel forward. Do three sets of 10. Repeat exercise with the other leg.

Hamstring to deep lunge (this page and next page)

Step-ups

Stand in front of a structure about two feet high, such as a bench or a double step. Step up onto the support, straighten your knees fully, and then step down. Do this at a steady pace. Add weights to your hands as you feel comfortable.

ANKLES AND FEET

Toe Raises

Stand with the balls of your feet and your toes on a thick book (such as a phone book). Hold onto a support. Lower your heels to the floor slowly. Raise yourself slowly as far as you can. Hold for eight to 10 seconds. Repeat 15 to 20 times.

Walking on Heels

While standing, lift your toes off the ground. Start walking on just your heels. Take 10 to 20 steps.

COOLDOWN

Cooling down is no less important than warming up as a part of your training routine. Whatever activity you are engaged in, you need to take adequate time to let your body make the transition from being stressed to being at rest. There is a physiological reason for this:

Intense athletic activities cause the buildup of lactic acid in your muscles, which contributes to muscle fatigue. Cooling down helps remove some of the lactic acid in your muscles.

Cooldown, like warm-up, gently reminds your body to switch gears. While the warm-up prepares your muscles and joints for increased activity, the cooldown helps your body relax. You can repeat the same stretches in cooldown that you performed in your warm-up. You'll find that it usually feels good to stretch after a tough workout. Your muscles are very warm, so it's easy to stretch, too. This extra stretching will improve your flexibility and will help prevent muscle cramps, improve circulation, and reduce soreness between workouts.

5 TUMBLING AND OTHER FLOOR EXERCISES

Tumbling is the foundation of gymnastics. Long before there was any apparatus, or even nice soft mats, athletes were practicing and perfecting the same basic skills we use today. And over the centuries just about every possible way of moving the body has been explored.

Tumbling shows you how to manipulate and move your arms, legs, head, and entire body. It teaches your muscles what to do to achieve a particular effect, and it generally gives you feel for gymnastics.

Later the same basic moves you learn on the tumbling mat will be transferred to the apparatus. It's often been said that gymnastics as a whole is essentially tumbling performed on various pieces of equipment. That's an oversimplification, of course, but there's a lot of truth in it.

The best way to learn any tumbling stunt is to take it in small steps. This cannot be stressed enough. Gymnastics skills build upon one another, so it's essential to follow the steps involved in mastering a trick in the exact order in which the steps are presented. By doing this you'll learn each stunt safely and avoid developing bad habits that may be difficult to correct later on.

GETTING INTO POSITION

While you perform skills, you will move into different positions. These are the pieces of the puzzle that you will put together to perform a skill. You will be asked to get into the stretch, squat, tuck, pike, straddle, and lunge positions at different times. Here's a brief description of the key positions.

Lunge position: The lunge is a basic starting position used for getting into various stunts. In spite of its name, it's really a static position. To take a lunge position, stand with your arms up over your head. Put one leg out in front of you about two feet and bend that leg at the knee. Lean forward, but keep your rear leg straight. This will mean you'll want to come up onto the ball of your rear leg foot. That's all there is to it.

You'll be using this position to get into handstands, cartwheels, handsprings, and lots of other stunts.

Tuck position: To learn the tuck, lie on your back and draw your legs up so your knees and thighs are against your chest and stomach. Your chin should be tucked down onto your chest, and your heels should be held in as near to your seat as possible. Next, put your hands on your knees and rock forward and backward very gently. Try to rock enough so that your head touches the mat as you go back and your heels just about touch the mat as you go forward.

Do this several times until you get used to the way it feels. Then take your hands off your knees and try to hold the same position with muscle power. Put your hands back by your ears, palms facing the mat, fingers close to your ears. Then rock back gently until your hands touch the mat and go forward as before.

Keep doing this until you become familiar with the way it feels. Then work on building up a little speed. Eventually you should rock fast enough to be able to roll forward and up onto your feet in a squat stand, with your hands in the same side-of-the-head position.

Straight or layout position: Stretch your arms and legs completely so that you form a straight line. This position is used when you are standing up and lying down. When standing up, your hands are stretched above your head.

Squat position: Bend down at the knees as low as you can until you're almost sitting down. Keep your feet close together in front of you to support your body.

Pike position: From a sitting position put your arms and legs straight in front of you.

Straddle position: Move your legs farther apart than your shoulders, as if you were riding a horse. When standing, your arms are spread apart, too.

SINGLE FORWARD ROLL

The forward roll is one of the most basic and important stunts in tumbling. It is used in almost all floor exercise routines of all levels and can be performed either as a lead-in to another stunt or as part of a series of forward rolls.

The ultimate goal is to begin in a standing position, bend down, tuck your head, and roll forward quickly enough to finish on your feet in a squat tuck position. You've already learned the second part. Here's how to do the first.

As always it's best to begin with a simple movement and gradually ease into the more difficult parts of the maneuver. First get down on all sixes—toes, knees, and hands—and practice bending your arms and touching your forehead to the mat in front of you.

Then come up to all fours—toes and hands—and practice bending your arms and neck so that the top of your head touches the mat. When you've done that a few times, inch your toes a bit closer to your hands and try to bend your arm and neck even more so that the back of your head touches the mat. After trying this a couple of times, do it once again and hold the position. Then walk your toes even closer to your hands until you roll forward and over onto your back. Don't push yourself. Just inch your toes forward and let gravity do the work.

Forward roll in a squat tuck (this page and next page)

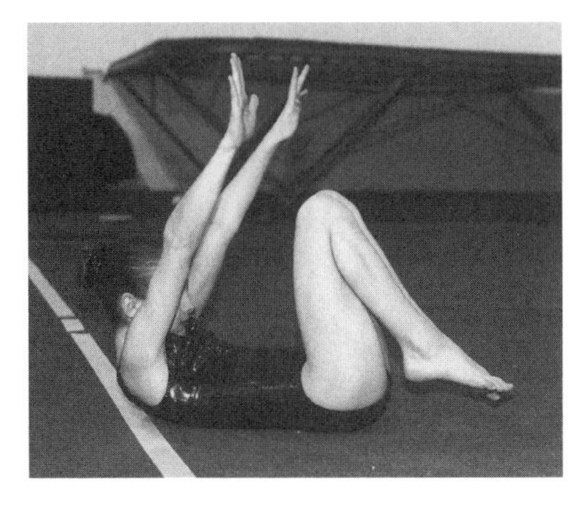

Once you've got the feel of rolling over, you can try to add a little speed with the idea of building up enough momentum to carry you on through the roll and up onto your feet. The key to a roll like this is to tuck your body into as small a ball as possible and to get the back of your head onto the mat. If you place the top of your head on the mat, you could get stuck in a headstand as you try to roll. Your knees and hips should be bent, and your chin should be tucked down onto your chest so that you're looking at your stomach.

To give yourself a little extra speed, you can push off with your toes. This will take some trial and error, but eventually you will be able to roll forward and onto your feet in a squat tuck position.

If you aren't able to make it to your feet at this point, it's OK to use your hands to help push your body up. However, you should try to do it without using your hands as soon as possible, as this is better form and because the forward roll will eventually lead to other stunts in your floor exercise routine in which using your hands will interfere with the transition.

Now you're ready to try the entire stunt. Begin from a standing position with your hands at your sides. Squat down and put your hands about two feet in front of you. Bend your elbows and roll forward quickly enough to come up onto your feet, then straighten up so that you're standing the same way you were at the start. With practice, you'll be able to make the entire stunt from beginning to end seem almost like a single smooth motion.

You should probably practice your tuck position with knees apart at first. This isn't good gymnastics form, but it prevents you from accidentally hitting your mouth with your knees. In fact, whenever you're learning a rolling or tucking movement, it's a good idea to begin with knees apart. Later when you've mastered it, you can bring your knees together into the correct gymnastic form.

If after several attempts you find that your roll isn't smooth or that you're still landing on your back, you may need a little help from someone else. Your instructor or an assistant can help you tuck properly by putting a hand on the back of your neck or helping you move your legs into a tighter, rounder tuck position.

TIPS

- Look at your belly button when you start the roll. That helps make sure you stay in a ball so you roll more easily. It also helps you stay aware of where you are throughout the roll.
- Stay in control when you roll. Roll as fast as you feel safe. Do not stop in the middle of the roll.
- Raise your arms as high as you can when your feet touch the floor coming out of the roll. That gives you the power you need to stand up and finish in the same stretch position in which you started.

VARIATIONS

- **Straddle forward roll:** Start with your legs spread apart in the straddle position. Put your hands in front of you on the mat between your legs. Tuck into a ball and move into the roll. Keep your legs apart as you roll so that you finish in the same straddle position.
- **Lunge forward roll:** Start with your front leg bent in the lunge position. Drag your back (straight) leg forward across the mat until both feet are even. Tuck into a ball and move into the roll.

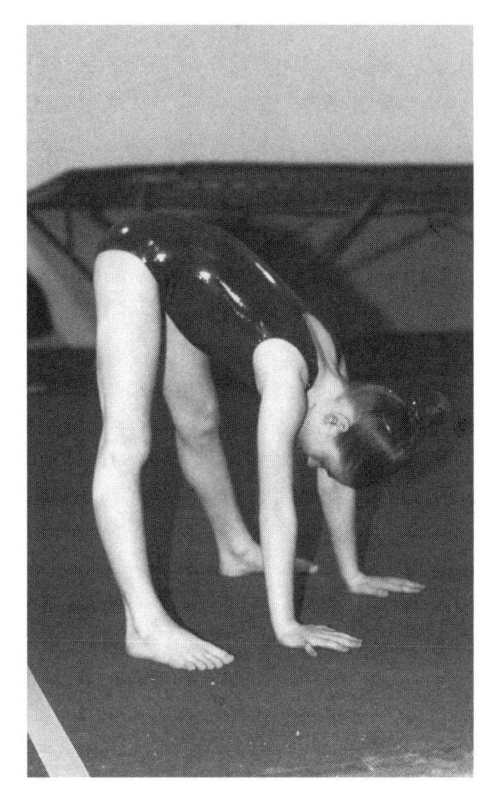

Straddle forward roll (above and right)

- **No-hands forward roll:** Start in the lunge position. Lower yourself to the mat by putting the back of your hands lightly on the mat. Tuck into a ball and roll without using your hands to push off. With practice, you won't have to use your hands at all.

THREE FORWARD ROLLS

As soon as you try this stunt you'll see why it was so important to learn how to do a forward roll without using your hands to push yourself up to a stand at the finish. The stunt begins and ends just as the single forward roll did, but in between you do three rolls instead of one. This means that as soon as you've finished one roll you've got to plant your hands in front of you to begin another one, something you couldn't do if your hands were busy pushing your body up to the squat position at the end of the first roll.

You begin this stunt by executing a forward roll just as before, only instead of rising to a stand as you come out of it, you immediately do a second and then a third roll. The three rolls should flow together almost as if they were one long, continuous motion. As you come out of the third roll, you raise your arms straight over your head, holding them close to your ears, and stand up straight. As soon as you're on your feet and standing stable, lower your arms to your sides to complete the trick.

Actually, even though it involves the same basic motion, this stunt is really three tricks. By doing it you learn how to start a roll from a stable position, how to keep a roll going, and how to stop a roll and then return to a stable position. These are skills that will be useful for cartwheels, handsprings and other tumbling stunts, as well as for forward rolls.

BACKWARD ROLLS

A backward roll is somewhat more difficult than the forward roll, but it isn't really much harder to master provided you use the right tumbling techniques. Begin by lying on your back in a tuck position. Rock back and forth on your back, gradually building up speed. Then, instead of trying to rock up and onto your feet as you did in learning the forward roll, try to go the other way. See if you can rock backward and pull your feet over your head. Using your hands for support, try to balance yourself in this "almost over" position for a moment. Then rock back down again. Be sure to keep your knees bent and, while you're learning the stunt, keep them apart as well.

Next, rock back a little faster and try to get your toes and/or knees to touch the mat on the other side. Then push up with your arms and slide your head out. You should find yourself on hands and knees.

After you've done this once, try to land on the balls of your feet without allowing your knees to touch the mat. You may have to rock faster to do this, and you'll have to push off more with your arms. Your goal is to arrive in a squat position, resting on just the balls of your feet and your hands. When you've got that down, simply bring your hands up beside your ears. You're now in the "ready position" for the next roll.

Now try the trick start from this squat position. Make yourself as round as you can while still keeping your balance. Then simply sit back and roll like a ball into the rest of the stunt. Be sure to avoid straightening your back at this point, for if you do, you won't be able to roll.

When you feel comfortable with this, try starting in a standing position. Stand more or less at attention with your arms raised overhead. Then in one smooth motion bend your knees, elbows, and body into a squat position and go into your backward roll as before.

As long as you remember to finish each roll in the "ready" position, you'll have no problem doing three backward rolls in succession. As you arrive on your feet after the third roll, finish the stunt by pushing off and rising to a stand, arms once again straight overhead. Once you're stable, slowly lower your arms to your sides.

As you've probably noticed, a lot of tumbling tricks (and other gymnastics stunts) begin with arms raised overhead and end with the arms being lowered to your sides. There are a couple of reasons for this. Probably the most important is the fact that by raising your arms at first, you are signaling the judges and spectators that you are about to begin your performance. And by lowering them at the end, you are giving notice that you have finished. It's something like the final chord in a piece of music, and it shows everyone that you are in complete control of your body.

There's also the fact that you naturally end up in a raised arm position as you finish many stunts—the end position of a back handspring, for example, or a dismount from the high bar. And often this position provides a good lead-in for stunts that are to follow, making for a smooth transition from one trick to another. That's why it's a good idea to make these arm movements a habit by practicing them right from the start.

One of the biggest problems with this stunt is remaining in a tuck position from the time you begin your roll until you get your body over. If you allow yourself to unfold, you won't roll smoothly and will have trouble getting your legs to come over and down. Concentrate on using your stomach muscles to keep yourself tucked.

As you bring your body over your head, your elbows should stay in close to your body. Resist the urge to let them go out to the sides. Only by keeping them in close will you be in the strongest position to push from.

If you don't have enough speed to go over smoothly, you will probably need some help from your instructor. Ask your instructor to stand near your feet at the beginning and walk forward as you rock up. He or she can then plant his or her feet on either side of you and, grabbing your hips, help lift you over. This will help you get the proper feel for the stunt. After a few assists, you'll probably be able to do it by yourself.

TIPS

- Beginners often use an incline mat. It takes a lot less strength and energy to do a backward roll downhill. Plus, it puts a lot less pressure on the head and neck, so it's safer, too.
- Look forward while rolling back. This helps you stay in the tuck position, prevents you from hitting your head on the floor, and helps you stay aware of where you are while upside down.

- Pretend you're holding a pizza with each hand before you start your roll. Try to smash the pizzas behind you as you roll backward. When your hands touch the mat, squash the pizzas even harder.
- Bring your feet over your shoulders as you roll. Do not shoot them into the air too early.
- Let your arms hit the mat first as you roll backward. This helps you finish the roll and protects your head and neck.
- Roll sideways over your shoulder and away from your spotter if you get stuck and can't finish the roll.

VARIATIONS

- **Backward roll, tuck position to straddle stand:** Start in the tuck position and finish in the straddle position.
- **Straddle backward roll:** Start and finish in the straddle position.
- **Straddle backward roll to straight leg stand:** Start in the straddle and finish standing with legs straight.
- **Straddle backward roll to pike:** Start in the straddle and finish in a sitting pike position.

BACKWARD EXTENSION ROLLS

The first step in learning this stunt is to do a backward roll but stop when you're exactly midway through it. You will be on your shoulders, legs and body tucked, hands on the mat by your ears. Now, instead of staying tucked, extend your legs so that they're pointing straight up toward the ceiling for a moment. Straighten your arms as much as possible and then land on your feet with your hands still on the floor.

Next, try the whole thing again, only this time thrust your legs out and up a little higher and harder and finish up as before. Practice this until you can get your body straightened up to a position near a handstand for a moment. Then bend at the waist and put your feet on the floor.

As a beginner, this is probably all you should do on this stunt at present. However, as you become more skilled, you'll want to be able to execute a backward extension roll in its most desirable form: You extend your legs and raise yourself to a full-fledged handstand, hold it for a moment, and then go into the handstand stepdown.

It's important to avoid going into a full handstand when you're learning this trick. In fact, the first few times you extend your legs you may not want to try for the halfway-between-ceiling-and-floor angle. In the beginning work on getting the feel of extending legs and straightening elbows simultaneously so you can push your head off the mat.

This trick will probably take a lot of strength at first. But as you become more confident and add a little speed, the momentum of extending your legs will help carry you up, and the stunt will be more a matter of coordination.

TUCKED HEAD BALANCE

Before you learn how to do a headstand, you need to learn what is called the tucked head balance. To perform this stunt, you begin in the same position used for learning the forward roll—that is, a squat with feet apart at shoulder width and hands 18 to 24 inches apart on the mat in front of you. Lower your head to the mat so that it touches six inches to a foot beyond your hands. Your head should touch the mat at a point somewhere between these two extremes, perhaps just slightly above the hairline. You shouldn't be on your forehead and you shouldn't be on the top of your head.

Your head and two hands will thus form a triangle, which according to science is the most stable way to support anything. What you're going to support is the rest of your body. To do this, slowly inch your toes toward your hands until you can place one of your bent knees against the upper portion of one of your arms. Then slowly raise the toes of that leg from the mat. When you've done that repeat the process with your other leg.

You may not be able to do it the first time. But you'll soon learn how to shift your weight so that you are in a balanced position with both feet off the mat. Hold that balance a moment or two, and then lower your toes to the mat and ease back into a squat.

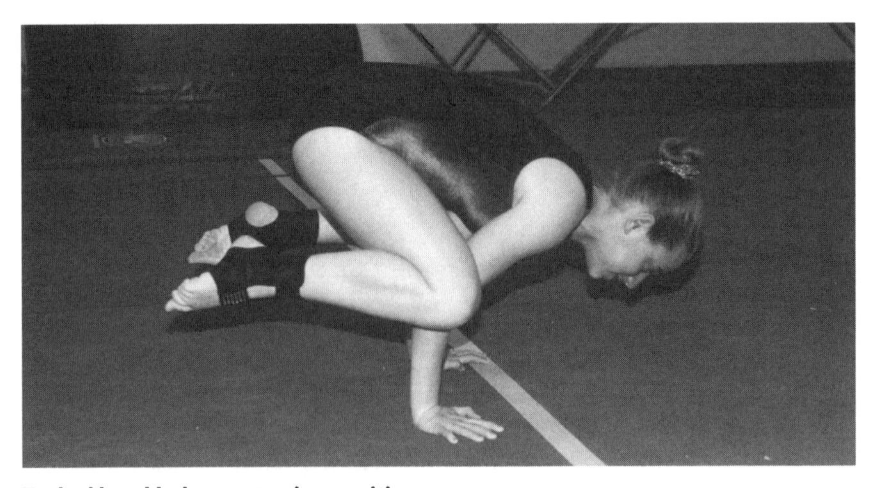

Tucked head balance, starting position

Doing a tucked head balance is an achievement in itself. But later you'll use the same technique to perform a regular headstand. A similar technique will also be used for doing a shoulder stand on the parallel bars.

HEADSTAND

To perform a headstand, begin by doing the tucked head balance. Then slowly lift your knees one inch off your elbows. This will take some weight shifting, so move very slowly until you have figured out what needs to be done. Your goal is to be able to balance in that position. Once you can do that, reverse the order of your movements and come back down. Then lift your head off the mat, rock back into the standard squat, and take a rest.

Now, start again, running through the entire sequence until you are once more balanced with your knees an inch off your elbows. Next, very slowly begin to push your feet up toward the ceiling. Push them until they are where you think is about halfway up. Then slowly lower them and return to the squat for a rest. Repeat this sequence two or three times until you can do it without shaking or wiggling.

Headstand

You're almost there. But before moving on to a full headstand, it's important to learn how to do a forward roll from the tucked head balance. The reason for this is simple: If you go too high, too fast, in the next stage of the headstand, you'll lose your balance and come crashing down like a tree. Knowing how to go into a forward roll when you lose your balance will prevent that.

So, begin by going to the tucked head balance with knees an inch off the elbows, only while you're moving your legs, push the rest of your body up at the same time. The idea is to raise your body just enough to allow you to tuck your head under. Then simply go into a forward roll.

As you bring your body over your head, your elbows should stay in close to your body. Resist the urge to let them go out to the sides. Only by keeping them in close will you be in the strongest position to push from.

Practice this several times. Try to make it something of a reflex action so that whenever you lose your balance in a headstand you do a forward roll almost without thinking.

Now you're ready to do a full headstand. Go to the tucked head balance with knees an inch off the elbows. Slowly raise your legs all the way up until your toes are pointed at the ceiling. When you get to that position, slowly straighten out all the parts—knees, hips, and so on—until you are perfectly balanced.

This isn't easy and will take some practice. But doing a successful headstand is a major skill and well worth the effort.

The main problem people have when learning this stunt is that they try to move their bodies too fast. It can't be emphasized enough: All motions must be slow so that you are on balance at all times. If you move too fast, you won't be able to shift your weight properly, and you'll end up off balance. When this happens, don't panic. Simply go into a forward roll or return to the tucked head balance, whichever is easier. Don't try to shoot your feet up to the ceiling, hoping to regain your balance once you're upside down.

It may be a good idea to have someone stand next to you as you learn this trick. That way if you begin to fall from the headstand position the spotter can grab your ankles, making sure you have enough time to get your head tucked for a forward roll.

TIPS

- Keep your back straight as possible. That helps support your weight safely.
- Balance in a position just short of holding yourself up straight. That way, you can hold the headstand steady by pushing up with your hands on the mat.

JUMP WITH A HALF TWIST

Your goal for this skill is to begin from a position similar to that used by swimmers doing a racing dive and then to shoot your arms over your head as you jump up into the air and do a half twist (either to the right or to the left). You should land on your feet facing the opposite direction and finish by lowering your arms to your sides.

Start by standing on the mat, knees bent and arms pointed out behind you. Your body should be bent forward slightly in a kind of half crouch. Swing your arms forward and upward until they are straight overhead with the upper arms in close to your ears. At the same time that you're swinging you arms, jump straight up and do a half twist in the air.

Don't jump really high at first. Try to jump only about an inch or so off the mat. That way you'll have less distance to fall if you should tip over to one side or another while in flight. Not all of your upward thrust has to come from your legs. Your arm swing can and should be used to increase your upward momentum, and it's well worth practicing since it is a central part of many advanced stunts.

As soon as you have done several one-inch jumps and successfully landed with your body under control, you can try for more height. There is no set optimum height for this stunt, but you should try for an inch or two more on each jump until you are able to point your toes while in the air. In fact, after you have the basic moves down, you should immediately begin working on your form. In this stunt that means keeping your knees straight, your legs together, and your toes pointed while you're in the air. This will create the kind of straight, pleasing line that judges look for in competition.

Although your knees should be straight while you're twisting, be sure to bend them slightly when you land. You should also bend a little at the waist as you come down. This will help absorb the shock. Then after you're stable, rise to a standing position.

Be sure to learn how to do a twist in both directions. After you've mastered the stunt turning one way, work on turning in the opposite direction. You should eventually be able to do a jump with a half twist to the right or to the left equally well.

In doing this stunt, you want to try to land in exactly the same spot that you began in. That is, you don't want to travel to the left or right of your starting position as you twist. This may not be possible at first, but with practice you'll discover how to eliminate or control those movements that throw you off course.

JUMP WITH A FULL TWIST

This stunt is similar to the previous one, except that you finish facing the same direction as when you began. The best way to master this stunt is to first master the half twist. Then try to twist a little more each time you jump. If you've learned the half twist correctly, getting enough height should be no problem. All you really have to do is learn to twist more quickly while you're in the air.

BACKBRIDGE

The backbridge is a very useful skill for several reasons. It is a basic tumbling position and a definite prerequisite for more advanced stunts like front and back handsprings. It's also a good warm-up exercise.

Begin by lying flat on your back. Bend your knees and bring your ankles up toward your seat. Put your hands behind your head, next to your ears, palms on the mat. Then push your stomach up toward the ceiling, straightening your arms and legs as you go. As you straighten your elbows, move your head back and down until you can see your hands on the floor.

When you first attempt this stunt, your feet should be about a shoulder's width apart. They should remain flat on the floor, pointed straight ahead. Later, after you feel comfortable forming the backbridge this way, try the more advanced version by doing it with your legs and ankles together.

If your shoulders and/or back are inflexible, you may not be able to do a backbridge right away. The solution is to do some stretching exercises before trying the stunt and to try doing a backbridge a few times each day until you gradually become more limber.

Handstand using the wall

HANDSTAND

You will use the handstand in every gymnastics event, so it is one of the most important skills to learn. It may take some time to learn, but the time will be well spent. Follow the progressions, and you'll find yourself enjoying kicking your feet up over your head.

Many gymnastics clubs use a wall to help you get the feel of kicking your feet into the handstand position. Stand with your back against the wall. Squat and put your hands on the mat. Put your feet up behind you on the wall as high as you can while still feeling safe. (Never move your feet higher than you feel comfortable because you have to support your body weight). Move your hands closer to the wall to raise your feet even higher. Put your legs together so that your arms and the rest of your body form a straight line. Walk your feet down the wall slowly so that you don't get hurt. Be prepared to do a forward roll or turn your body away from the wall if your feet come off the wall and you lose your balance.

Handstand step-down and a complete handstand (above, below, and next page)

HANDSTAND STEP-DOWN

This is a stunt all by itself, but it's also a great way to prepare for other stunts involving a full handstand. Start by getting into the same position as when beginning a push-up: palms on the mat, arms extended straight, legs straight, feet up on their toes. Bring one foot up closer to your hands, bending the knee. Now you are in the lunge position, and the bent leg is your support leg.

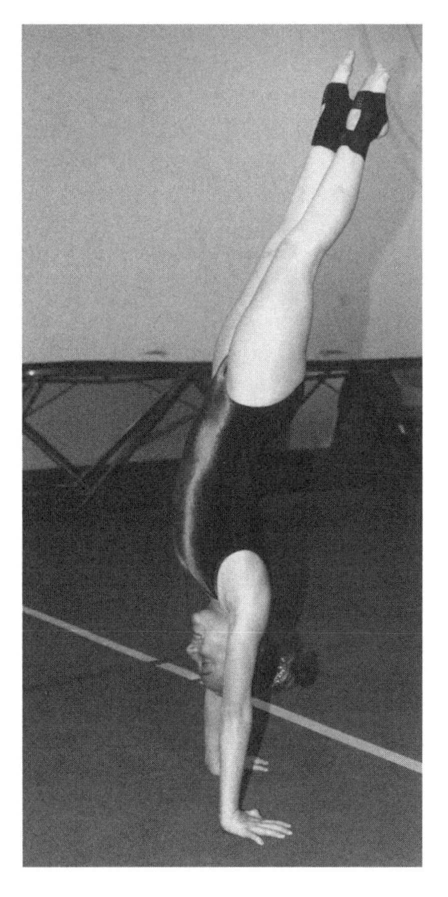

Slowly lift your other leg, still keeping it straight with toes pointed, up off the mat.

Next, take your stand, step forward into the lunge, and then slowly move down so that your hands are on the mat and you're in the beginning push-up position. Notice that the leg brought forward for the lunge will now be your support leg. Pause for a moment, and then bring your straight leg up and perform the stunt as before.

The pause is important at this stage because it counteracts the tendency to raise the straight leg too soon. Don't bring that leg up until your hands are properly placed on the mat. As you get better at the trick you can eliminate the pause and work toward a smoother execution. Just remember to take it slowly. Don't try to go too fast at first.

You may have to experiment a little until you learn how much strength is needed to keep your arms straight. By making sure that your arms are straight and that your shoulders are always directly over your hands, you'll not only have good form, but you will also make the trick easier. When your bones are lined up correctly, you can support yourself without much effort.

Keep your head in its original position at all times. Don't tuck it. You ought to be able to see your fingers and hands all during the stunt.

Finally, be sure not to go into a handstand. You want to come close to it but not completely into it.

Raise your straight leg a few inches at first, then return it to the floor. Repeat this leg lift with a bit more speed, trying to get it a little higher each time, until the momentum forces your support foot to lift off the mat slightly. When you've done that, try to hold your airborne position for a second before coming down. Try to come down with your support foot in exactly the same spot.

The straight leg should be absolutely straight with toes pointed until it touches the mat. The idea is eventually to be able to get your straight leg up to the angle shown in the accompanying photograph, to hold the position very briefly, and then to come back down. However, you don't want to raise your leg so high that you pull yourself into a handstand.

Once you've mastered the trick with one leg, reverse positions and try it with the other leg. Then try getting into the stunt from a standing position.

HANDSTAND (COMPLETE)

You've just learned the handstand step-down. Once you've mastered it, you'll be ready to move on to a complete handstand. To help you learn this stunt, it's a good idea to have a fellow student or your instructor standing by.

Begin by performing the handstand step-down several times, trying to kick your straight leg higher each time. Then try to kick it high enough to pull the trunk of your body into a vertical position. The leg itself should stop somewhere past a vertical line drawn through your trunk, while your support leg rises to a spot about the same distance on the other side of that line. This is a split-leg position.

You should try to balance in the split-leg position for a moment. However, if you feel yourself falling back down, simply lower your rear leg and do a handstand step-down. If you find that you've kicked your straight leg too far and are about to fall forward, your instructor or spotter will hold your legs to ease your landing.

Once you are able to balance in the split-leg position for about two seconds, try to join your legs together so that your whole body is vertical. By holding you in both this position and in the split-leg position, your instructor or spotter can help you get accustomed to the stunt and to what your muscles must do to perform it on their own.

When you've mastered the handstand and feel confident of your ability to perform it without assistance, practice beginning the stunt from a stand. From a stand, go into a lunge and lower yourself to the handstand step-down position. Kick your straight leg up and follow with your support leg so that you're in the split-leg position. Then join your legs for a finished handstand. Complete the stunt by resplitting your legs and performing a handstand step-down.

TIPS

- Don't worry about the height of your leg kick when you first try a handstand. With even a slight kick, you'll start to feel what it's like to put your body over your hands. Work hard when you do your strength exercises. You'll progress with practice.
- Put your hands as far from your front (lunge) foot as possible. That way you can slowly swing up into the handstand.

- Keep your head steady throughout the handstand.
- Look at a spot at the floor directly between your hands.
- Balance in a position just past the vertical position. That way you can keep your balance when you push hard on the mat with your hands.
- Count for three seconds once you have successfully kicked to a handstand.

HANDSTAND TO FORWARD ROLL

Linking a handstand and a forward roll together can be very useful in a floor exercise routine, where it's important to keep moving in one direction or another as you cover the area.

With your instructor or a spotter standing by, do the handstand you just learned. Once you're balanced with your legs together overhead, the spotter will hold both your legs to help support some of your weight. This will give you a chance to tuck your head, with chin on chest, so that your shoulders are nearly touching the mat.

Now the spotter will lower you gently as you complete your tuck and go into a forward roll. You should come out of the roll as usual, arriving in a squat with hands up by your ears. Then you simply rise to a full stand.

The key to this stunt is to learn how and when to tuck your head before going into the roll. This will take some work, but as you get better at it, the instructor or spotter will gradually reduce his assistance until you can do it by yourself.

Once you can do a single handstand-forward roll, it's easy to do two in a row. Begin the first handstand-forward roll by assuming the lunge position. Put your hands on the mat. Swing up to a handstand, joining the legs. Tuck your head and lower your shoulders. Do a forward roll up to your feet. Rise to a stand with arms overhead. Swing arms rearward, down and forward as you go into the lunge. Then repeat.

You'll probably have a tendency at first to try to do a forward roll before you've gotten yourself into a complete handstand. Do your best to resist this. If you try to do a forward roll before your legs are all the way up, you may literally fall flat on your face. So be mentally prepared to do the handstand step-down if you try for a full handstand and don't make it. This will get you out of trouble safely.

CANDLESTICK

The candlestick is a basic stunt that is performed in floor exercise as well as on the balance beam. It can be performed in combination with a backbridge or roll-up. From a standing position with your arms fully extended straight over your head, bend your knees into a tuck-sit position, and roll backward into the candlestick position—legs pointing straight upward with toes pointing at the ceiling and your body supported by your neck, shoulders, and arms. Try to keep your arms extended as you bring them downward and finish with them flat on the mat with palms down just in front of your buttocks.

Candlestick

RELEVÉ WALK

Walking in relevé simply means walking on the balls of your feet. Begin by pointing your left foot forward on the floor. Lift your right foot and step forward, landing on the ball of your foot. Alternate left and right in this manner, finishing by bringing your feet together in relevé and lowering the heels to the mat in a straight stand.

LEG SWING

Step forward with your left leg, keeping it straight. Swing your right leg forward and upward until it is parallel to the mat. Bring the leg down so your right foot is in front of your left. Repeat the maneuver, this time raising your left leg. Keep your hips squared throughout the exercise.

SPLIT JUMP

With both legs in demi-plié, push off the floor extending your legs through the hips, knees, ankles, and toes. Keeping your legs straight, separate them a minimum of 45 degrees with your right leg forward and your left leg back. Bring your legs back together for the landing, so that you land on both feet side by side and your legs slightly flexed. This position is called "demi-plié." Finish in a straight stand.

PLIÉ, COUPÉ WALK

Plié is a French term for bending of the knees. *Coupé* describes a position in which your leg is bent with the toe pointed on or behind your ankle, depending on the position of the support leg.

To perform the plié, coupé walk, point your left foot forward on the mat.

Split jump

Plié, coupé walk (this page and next)

Your arms should be pointing out to the sides, parallel to the floor. Push off your right foot at the same time you are bending your left knee and moving forward onto your left foot (the left foot goes from relevé to flat). Extend your right leg with the right foot pointed behind you as your weight transfers to your left foot. Bend your right knee forward and pull your right foot forward to touch your left ankle (forward coupé position). Extend your right leg forward on the mat, and repeat the movement with your right leg in front.

FORWARD CHASSÉ

With your arms pointing out to the sides and parallel to the floor, move forward with your right leg in demi-plié. Slide the left foot forward through fourth position demi-plié (knees slightly bent, feet placed one in front of the other, approximately 12 to 18 inches apart, with the toes turned out). Push off with both feet and close your right foot behind your left foot in midair so that the heel of your left foot presses against the front of your right foot. This is a forward chassé left. Land in demi-plié on your right leg and repeat the movement, this time stepping forward with your left leg in demi-plié and performing a forward chassé right (heel of your right foot pressing against the front of your left foot).

BACKWARD CHASSÉ

With both legs in demi-plié, slide your left foot backward through fourth position demi-plié (knees slightly bent, feet placed one in front of the other, approximately 12 to 18 inches apart, with the toes turned out). Push off the floor with both feet, and bring your right foot in front of your left foot in midair so that your right heel is pressed against the front of your left foot. This is a backward chassé left. Land in demi-plié on your right leg, then step backward on your left leg in demi-plié and slide your right foot backward through fourth position demi-plié. Repeat the movement, this time performing a backward chassé right (left heel pressed against the front of your right foot).

FRONT SCALE

Balancing feats and tricks are a prime element of floor exercise competition. And while by definition they are all static positions, they are anything but easy to do. Most balanced positions, or "scales," require a lot of strength and flexibility.

Front scale (above and below)

The front scale is a basic floor exercise stunt. You begin by standing with arms overhead and then step into the lunge position. At this point a line drawn through your back leg, hips, shoulders, arms, and fingers should be absolutely straight. Now lift your rear leg off the floor, toes pointed, and try balancing on your bent leg.

When you can do that, try to straighten your bent leg as you tilt your body forward into a horizontal position. Keep your arms at your sides and pointed back, and look straight ahead.

This is not easy to do, but once accustomed to the basic position, you should try to perfect it. Your goal should be to balance for several seconds with your rear leg, your hips, head, hands, and arms all in the same horizontal plane. As you practice, ask a friend to help you by standing back and telling you whether everything is lined up properly. Eventually you'll get so you will know whether or not you're on target just by the way it feels.

You can come out of the front scale by lowering your rear leg and bringing yourself up to a stand. But you can also use it as a link to some other stunt. For example you could bend your support leg slightly, put your hands on the mat, and go into a handstand forward roll. Or, to make things even more elaborate, you could begin from a stand, lunge into a handstand forward roll, come out of the roll rising to your feet and into a front scale, hold it for a few seconds, then go into another handstand forward roll.

FORWARD ROLL TO A ONE-LEGGED STAND

Remember the part of the forward roll in which you're on your back, legs tucked, ready to come up to a squat? Well, instead of keeping both legs tucked, straighten one of them, pointing the toe, and try to arrive in a squat supported by the tucked leg. The straight leg will be out in front of you, and you'll look as though you're in the middle of a Russian dance.

Now for the really hard part. From this position try to straighten your support leg, rising to a stand, while keeping the straight leg out in front of you. This will demonstrate strength and flexibility and requires a lot of both.

Once you can do this, you can easily lean forward and touch down with your straight leg. By flexing the support leg at the same time, you'll find yourself in the lunge position, ready to go into some other stunt.

At first getting up on one leg with the other held straight out in front will be hard enough. But you can make the stunt even more difficult by trying it with your arms held straight overhead and your front leg held even higher.

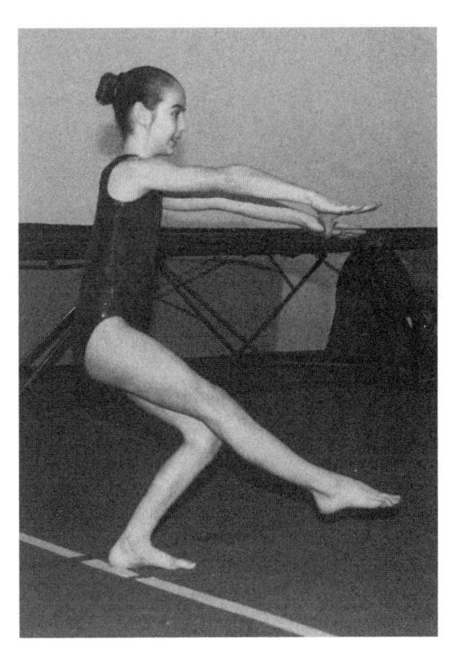

Forward roll to a one-legged stand (above and right)

THE HURDLE

The hurdle is simply a little skip step taken at the beginning of a stunt to give yourself a little speed. Begin by standing with your arms at your sides. Then raise your arms straight forward and up until they're overhead. At the same time, raise your left leg, knee straight and toes pointed. Done with enough speed, the momentum of these two actions will help pull you into a forward skip on your right foot.

As your right foot hits the mat after the skip, step down with your left foot and go into a cartwheel or a roundoff (see below). You'll probably find that the little bit of extra forward motion provided by the hurdle makes these stunts easier.

When you're comfortable doing the hurdle, try adding a little step. Step forward with your right foot and as you bring your left leg forward, raise your arms and do a hurdle. Then go into a cartwheel or a roundoff. This will further increase your speed.

If you like, you can add two more steps as well. But you'll have to stop there since in gymnastics even the most difficult tumbling stunts are never preceded by more than three steps and a hurdle. Be sure to learn the hurdle and steps on both legs.

CARTWHEELS

Although considered a beginning stunt, a cartwheel is still a pretty impressive skill. It's a little difficult to do, so it's worth reemphasizing the importance of following the proper progression of steps as you learn it. Follow the steps as they are presented here, and you'll be able to do the stunt safely without any problem.

As you stand facing down the mat, try to picture yourself at the end of a straight line running right out in front of you. Shift slightly to the right before starting so that the line is next to your left foot. We'll assume you will be swinging your right leg up first, so as you go into a lunge, step forward with your left leg.

Lunge down as though you were going to do a handstand, but plant your

Cartwheel (this page and next page)

left hand on that imaginary line. Your right hand should be planted about a shoulder's width from your left. This means you'll shift slightly to the right as you lunge. Swing your right leg up and then bring up your left leg. You'll be in a handstand, but your legs should be split, right leg leaning forward, left leg leaning back. If you find you can't make the split-leg handstand at first, just ease back down onto your left leg and try again.

When you arrive at the handstand, begin to lean forward a bit. Quickly pick up your right hand and plant it on the line about a shoulder's width in front of your left hand. You'll pivot slightly on your left hand as your body twists around.

Next, put your right leg on the line even farther out than your right hand. You'll be moving it down and sideways and the action will tend to pull your body upright. You can help things along by pushing off a little with your left hand. The left leg, of course, follows naturally and should also be placed on the line.

The explanation takes a lot longer than the stunt itself. And while the trick does not look like a cartwheel yet, mastering it is an important preliminary step.

The next step is to stand with your left foot on the imaginary line. Lunge forward and plant your left hand on the line in front of your left foot. Be sure to keep your right arm stretched out above your left arm. Now swing your right leg up and at the same time place your right hand on the line. You'll pivot slightly on your left hand as before.

See if you can swing your right leg all the way through—past the vertical position so that it is in front of you—and place it on the line. This will look more like a real cartwheel.

Now push off with your left hand and then with the right. Bring your left leg down and onto the line and pivot so that you are facing back the way you came. Notice that your right leg will now be the forward leg. This makes it easy to again go into a lunge and do another cartwheel, only this time you'll start by planting your right hand on the line and swinging your left leg up first.

When you've done this sequence a number of times, you'll be ready for the complete trick. Begin with arms overhead, step forward into a lunge with your left leg, pass smoothly through the lunge and into a cartwheel. You will end up in a lunge position facing back the way you came. Instead of holding that pose, straighten up and step back onto your rear (left) foot and join your legs. Your hands will still be over your head. From here go right into a lunge stepping forward with your right leg, and do another cartwheel.

This is a perfectly acceptable mini-routine often used in floor-exercise competition. Usually it does not matter which cartwheel (right leg or left leg) you execute first as long as you demonstrate both of them.

The second type of cartwheel is the one most people think of when they hear the word. It is easy to learn once you've mastered the handstand type. Begin by standing, arms overhead, with your left side to the imaginary line. Swing your left leg straight out to the left and plant it on the line. Then quickly bring your left arm and shoulder down so you can plant your left hand about 18 inches farther along the line than your foot. You'll have to flex at the waist, and the movement will bring your right leg up off the mat. Try to keep your arms and legs rather stiff.

Next place your right hand on the line about a shoulder's width from your left hand. While you're doing this, keep your eyes focused on the mat on a spot between your hands. Moving your right arm into position will help you bring your right leg up and through. And that will help you bring up your left leg.

Finish up by pushing off a little with your left hand and bringing your right leg down and onto the line. Again, keep your arms and legs stiff so you can use them like the spokes of a wheel. You should arrive in a stand with your arms over your head, which makes it very easy to continue with another cartwheel in the same direction or do one that will carry you back the way you came.

Either type of cartwheel is acceptable for competition, unless you must do a compulsory routine that specifies a certain type. The second type, though, is better suited for continuing on in the same direction, as when you're doing a series of stunts that carry you across the mat.

Speed and momentum can be a big help in getting your body up, over the top, and down on the other side, but try to go slowly at first. You don't, for instance, have to hurry through the lunge position when doing the first type of cartwheel. Just try to make it a smooth motion at first. You can add some speed later. And remember, you want to be able eventually to execute both types of cartwheels in both directions equally well.

TIPS

- Your gymnastics club may use brightly colored mats or blocks to help you learn a cartwheel. The colored mats or chalk are a great guide to show you where to place your hands and feet.
- Count the four steps of the cartwheel to establish a rhythm: hand, hand, foot, foot.
- Place the first hand down as far away from your lunge foot as possible. The farther away you place your lunge foot, the easier the cartwheel will be. Remember that a larger wheel with longer spokes moves faster, and a faster cartwheel may be scarier. Don't

go too fast. Instead try to stay smooth and in control from the beginning to the end of your cartwheel.
- Place the second hand as far from the first hand as possible.
- Look for the floor without raising your head.

VARIATIONS

- **Cartwheel quarter-turn in:** Finish by facing (into) the direction you started from.
- **Cartwheel quarter-turn out:** Finish by facing (out) the same direction you started.
- **Opposite-side cartwheel:** This cartwheel is difficult; it's hard to keep your body awareness.
- **Series of cartwheels:** Perform two or more cartwheels without stopping.

TWO ONE-HANDED CARTWHEELS

It seems that a stunt is no sooner invented than someone comes up with a way to make it more challenging. That's the fun of gymnastics. The one-handed cartwheel is a case in point.

One-handed cartwheel (above, right, and top of next page)

For this stunt use the type of cartwheel done from a lunge. Stand next to the imaginary line. Lunge onto your left leg and place your left hand on the line. Then kick over so quickly that you don't have to put your right hand on the mat and, pushing off with your left hand, land in a lunge (right leg forward) facing the opposite direction. Repeat the trick by going back using your right hand instead of your left. This is called a near-arm cartwheel.

The secret is to swing up and over the first leg much faster than in a two-handed cartwheel. You need plenty of momentum to carry you over. It is also important to swing that leg straight up and over the top so that you land straight on the line. If you swing crooked, you'll land off balance.

At first, keep your right hand near the floor. That way you can use it if you have to. But later, if you really want to fancy up the stunt, try to keep your right arm stretched out to the side.

This is a difficult trick for most people, but once you can perform it, you might want to make it more difficult still. Begin by placing both hands near the line at the same time. Then, when the left hand is only an inch from the mat, take it away and use your right hand instead. You should place your right hand on the spot that would otherwise be occupied by your left hand as you swing your left arm away to the side. You'll then be doing a cartwheel on your far arm, and you'll have to move even more quickly than before to get your body over.

When doing a far-arm cartwheel, you may feel like taking your left arm away too soon. Counteract this tendency by concentrating on putting both hands near the line at the same time. This is also a good safety measure since your left hand will be there to help if you do not have enough speed to complete the trick on one hand.

Be sure to practice the one-handed cartwheel in either direction, and work on a smooth transition between the first and second cartwheels in the sequence.

Bridge kickover (above and both below)

BRIDGE KICKOVER

From a lying position with your knees bent and hands on either side of your head, push against the floor and arch your back. This puts you in a bridge position. Keep your eyes looking overhead and your legs straight. Kick one leg up and move it toward your head, then raise the other leg and have it follow the other overhead. You will briefly pass through a handstand position. Continue moving the legs past your head and onto the mat. Keep the first leg straight as you continue to move the upper body upward into a standing position. Keep the hands and arms high overhead and point the left foot behind on the floor. Lower the heel of the second foot and half-bend the other leg to finish in a right lunge, pressing the right knee and both hips forward.

THE ROUNDOFF

The roundoff is a key stunt in floor exercise because it can be used to convert a forward run into a backward movement. It begins like the cartwheel and can be done to either side. Here you'll learn it from a standing position and going to the right.

Begin as in a cartwheel, by imagining yourself straddling an invisible line running down the mat. Step into a lunge with your left foot and, bending at the waist, plant your left hand on the line. Follow with your right hand as you swing your right leg up into the air. The fingers of your left hand should cross the line at a right angle, but your right hand should point more or less back toward the direction you were lunging from.

This will cause your body to twist as in a cartwheel, and as this happens bring your left leg up to join your right. You'll now be in a handstand, legs together, directly above the line.

To complete the stunt, bring your legs down so that they land on the line with toes pointing back toward the place you began. Your body will thus twist some more as you come down to stand facing the opposite direction from which you started.

In its final form, the stunt should be done smoothly from beginning to end; that is, you should pass through the handstand without holding the position. Once you can do a roundoff in one direction, go on and perfect it in the other direction. You may also want to work on connecting the roundoff to another stunt by immediately going into a backward roll at the finish.

FRONT LIMBER

With arms fully extended above your head, step forward with your left leg, keeping the leg straight. Kick your right leg to a point parallel to the floor, then take a long step forward onto the ball of your right foot, keeping your right leg straight and lifting your leg backward and upward. Keeping your body straight, lower your torso and continue to lift your left leg backward and upward, and place your hands shoulder-width apart on the mat. Push off with your right leg and move into a handstand with your legs together. Lower your legs over your head into a bridge position with your feet flat on the floor and your legs shoulder-width apart. Push off with your hands, push your hips and thighs forward, and stand up to finish in a straight stand.

FLIC-FLAC

This is also known as a flip-flop or back handspring. It is used in a majority of tumbling passes on the floor exercise. It's also used a great deal on the balance beam.

Standing straight with arms fully extended above your head, lean backward and bend your knees, then extend your knees and jump backward onto your hands in a stretched body position. Push off the floor using your arms and shoulders while snapping your legs under, and land on both feet in an upright hollow body position. Rebound by jumping up in a stretched body position, and land in demi-plié.

Swing your arms downward as you bend your knees, then back upward as you jump backward. Keep your arms high on the rebound, then bring them down at a 45-degree angle to vertical on landing before finishing in a straight stand.

6 VAULTING

If you've ever vaulted over a fence or a fallen log or played leapfrog when you were younger, you know how much fun it can be. In fact vaulting is probably the one event with which you've had the most experience outside the gym, possibly even more than with tumbling.

That's not surprising, for vaulting is a pretty natural human movement, one that people have been executing and enjoying for thousands of years, as in the ancient Mediterranean kingdom of Crete, where bull leaping was a very popular exhibition sport. The essence of the vault is flight, achieved these days by a springboard to the vaulting table (preflight) and from the vaulting table to the landing (postflight). Between them the gymnast does what is basically a handspring or a cartwheel.

Flight requires height, and height requires speed, so the rules allow you to start your approach anywhere within 20 meters of the vaulting table. The rules also require you to land in perfect control of your body. Naturally, you are expected to flex your knees to absorb the shock of landing. But you're not supposed to squat too far, take a step, or do anything else demonstrating lack of balance.

Within this overall framework, a gymnast can do a lot of different things to make a vault more difficult and impressive. During the preflight, for instance, it is possible to do a half or full twist. On the way down, during the postflight, twists, saltos (of many varieties), and other maneuvers are possible.

A gymnast is scored on the basis of his or her performance in each of the two flight components. The rules assign each vault a particular level of difficulty for each age group and stipulate the maximum number of points a gymnast can earn for each one. The higher the difficulty level, the higher the points, up to a maximum of 10.0.

The vault is the only event that does not have requirements regarding the number and difficulty of the stunts a competitor must perform. This is because the vault is really just one stunt. That makes the vault the single most exciting moment in gymnastics. It calls for a single burst of lightning-fast reflexes, and then it's over. If you make a mistake in the other events, you usually have time to recover and continue with your routine. In the vault, however, the whole thing is over before you have a chance to recover.

BASIC SKILLS: RUN, JUMP, AND LAND

The basic skills of vaulting may seem pretty simple. You run, then you jump onto the springboard, which is called the vaulting board. Your run combined with the power of your jump and the spring from the board will launch you into the air. It's important to learn how to land safely.

Vaulting board

You will probably begin to learn by jumping onto a padded trapezoid-shaped vault that is about the same height as the vaulting board. Many beginners are afraid of jumping high because they're worried about landing. You will practice landing from different heights. The trapezoid vault is a great teaching tool because it is made of blocks that can be adjusted.

All gymnastics is based on step-by-step progressions. In vaulting every one of your steps is especially important. You have to learn the proper footwork, and you will practice running and jumping many times before you even attempt a vault. When you find the right footwork and gain confidence in your jumping, your instructor can increase the height of the trapezoid vault. Be patient.

Vaulting table, or block

It takes time to learn how to coordinate your run and jump into one smooth motion.

The height of your jump, which gymnasts call "amplitude," puts you in the position to vault. You must soar high enough to put your hands on the vaulting table, which used to be called the "horse" and is now known as the "block." You use your hands to push hard against the vaulting table. Advanced gymnasts use the block to do handsprings, cartwheels, and many other vaults. But before you think about amplitude and different vaults, you have to master the basics.

RUNNING

You need to get a running start to be able to vault. It is important to run with good form, and your instructor will help you to achieve this. Run on your toes, stride the same each time, and pump your arms close to your body. In class, as an exercise, you may race against others, but it's not important who wins. You should feel comfortable, confident, and fully in control as you approach the vaulting board. Always focus on a spot on the vaulting board. When you jump from the board, look at the spot on the trapezoid vault where you want to land, and later, the spot on the block from where you want to push off.

Approaching and jumping from the vaulting board (above and right)

JUMPING

Basic board jumping is very important in learning how to vault properly, but learning how to jump properly is not as easy as it may seem. You have to learn how to take your final step onto the top of the springboard, which is called the "hurdle." That puts you into the position to jump with both feet and spring up into the air. It might take a while before you learn how to jump properly from the board. You're supposed to jump only once on the board, but often beginners try to jump twice, or jump with one foot, or jump with two feet before they even reach the board.

USING THE SPRINGBOARD

Up to now, you've been doing everything either from a stand or from a short run. You may or may not have been using a springboard. At this point, however, it is important to learn how to use one properly. As you may have already discovered, a springboard is unlike any other device you've ever jumped from. Nowhere near as bouncy as even the stiffest diving boards, a springboard is designed to provide a short, quick concentrated lift, and there's a special technique for using one.

You run to the vaulting board and jump onto it with both feet. The jump must be as low and quick as you can make it, and your knees and ankles should be only slightly bent. Because of the way the spring is conveyed to your body, your legs must be very tense. If they're too flexible, the spring won't be able to travel up and into your body. You should hit the board on the toes and balls of your feet.

To get used to the board, place it so that you can stand up on it and reach out to touch the vaulting table without bending at the waist. Approach the board with a gentle three- to five-step run. As you become more confident, you can circle your arms up to get a little extra height.

VAULTING

You will start by jumping onto the trapezoid vault and landing on your feet. Next you will learn how to push off from the trapezoid with your hands to vault over it. A strong push-off launches you high into the air for your vault.

The quality of your push-off depends on the strength of your arms, shoulders, and hands. As your confidence, strength, and jumping technique continue to improve, your instructor may allow you to practice jumping over the vaulting table. You will practice the following progressions.

Vaulting

Landing

LANDING

Bend your knees slightly to absorb the impact of landing. Try to land on the balls of your feet, and then you'll automatically lower your heels. Keep your feet shoulder-width apart. Move your arms slightly forward and slightly out to the sides to improve your balance. Keep your head steady and look straight ahead.

Your goal is to hold this position without moving, or "stick" your landing. The faster you run and move through the air, the more your feet should land in front of you to allow you to stick in the same spot.

STRAIGHT JUMP ONTO MAT STACK

One way to practice running, jumping, and landing is to do a straight jump onto a mat stack. To do this, have a landing area of mats stacked about 12 inches high close to the springboard. Run seven to nine steps, hurdle onto the board, and jump off the board in a hollow-body position with your abdominals tight. (In the hollow-body position your arms should be raised above your head, your head should be slightly forward, and your chest should be rounded inward. You can practice this position by lying on the floor, making sure to keep your lower back in contact with the floor.) Land in a demi-plié in a controlled position.

FORWARD ROLL ONTO MAT STACK (WAIST HEIGHT)

This is another beginning exercise that gets you used to running, jumping, and landing. With the mats stacked at waist height near the springboard, run seven to nine steps, hurdle onto the board and reach forward to place your hands on the mat while maintaining a hollow-body position. Bend your arms (with elbows tucked in), tuck your head to your chest and execute a forward roll into a tucked position. Finish in a straight stand.

SQUAT ON, JUMP OFF

This isn't a real vault, but it is a valuable skill to learn nonetheless. Before you begin get into a push-up position on the floor and practice snapping your legs up into a squat with your hands still on the mat. This is basically the same movement you'll be doing on the vaulting table.

Next place your hands in the center of the vaulting table a little more than a shoulder's width apart. Then jump up with both feet and land on the table in a squat, feet between your arms. From this position, pick up your hands and push off with your feet as you jump down on the other side.

You should have an instructor or spotter help you with this stunt in case you don't get your feet on the vaulting table or in case they slip off. Also, be careful not to bring your feet through without touching the vaulting table, as you would land on the other side with both arms still on the table and stretched behind at a painful angle.

As you become more confident, try adding more stretch when you jump off. Jump up as straight as you can, thrusting your arms overhead and keeping them there as you land on both feet. You should bend at the knees to cushion the shock of landing, but right from the start you should work on control. Try to land without having to take an extra step or being off balance, pause for a moment, then lower your arms to your sides.

As you get better and better, add a variation or two. Try doing a half twist in the air before landing. Then try for a full twist. Later you can add a short run and try to bring your legs through without touching the vaulting table. This means you'll be going over the table in a squat vault, and the caution about allowing your arms to remain back on the table is the same as before. Be sure to push off with your hands as you leave the table, stretch your body to its full length, and raise your arms overhead.

Pike on, jump off

PIKE ON, JUMP OFF

Use a seven- or nine-step run-up, hurdle onto the board, and place your hands (with arms extended) on the trapezoidal vaulting table, keeping a hollow-body position. Press down with your hands while lifting your hips into a pike position. With legs still extended (a slight bend is OK), bring your feet on top of the vaulting table between your arms. Jump to a straight hollow-body position with arms extended overhead, and land in demi-plié.

HANDSPRING VAULT

The handspring is a basic vaulting skill. Nearly everything else is a variation of it created by adding twists during the preflight and assorted saltos and twists during the postflight.

You will probably learn the handspring on mats first, and then follow a gradual progression designed to make it as easy and as safe as possible. Make sure you follow your instructor's advice, and don't jump ahead until you have mastered the required techniques. Following are a few preliminary exercises you may perform to prepare you for doing a handspring vault.

Handstand Block

For this exercise you'll need the springboard and at least 16 inches of mats for a landing area. Set the board close to the mats, and take a one-to three-step run-up. Swing your arms in an exaggerated motion from low in back of you to high in front of you, and place your hands on the board while pushing off the floor with your front leg and kicking your back leg upward and backward. Keeping your arms straight and your body in a straight hollow position, push off the board with your hands.

Your legs should be together with your hips extended. Let your body go past vertical and rotate to land on your back on the mats. You may want to have a spotter assist you in landing.

Jump to Handstand onto a Raised Mat Surface

Set up the springboard close to a mat stack that is at least 32 inches high. Take a seven- or nine-step run-up and hurdle onto the board. Jump off the board with your arms and body extended, and reach for the mats with your hands. Staying extended, driving your legs upward to a handstand position with your arms straight. Keep your head neutral (neither tucked nor arched) and focus on your hands. Keep your legs together and your body in a straight hollow position. Land in a straight lying position on your back.

VARIATIONS

- Instead of landing on your back, use your tumbling log roll to twist over onto your stomach before you hit the mat. Here's a word of caution, though: Don't twist unless you are quite certain you can land perfectly flat. If you land on your stomach with one end of your body higher than the other, your back will bend, and that can be painful.
- If you can successfully twist onto your stomach, try for a full twist so that you land on your back.

Handspring vault

Handspring Vault

Take a good strong run-up and accelerate into the hurdle. Swing your arms from your sides forward and upward until they are in shoulder extension, keeping your eyes focused on your hands. Jump off the board, keeping a hollow-body position with your legs together and your hips extended. Drive your heels backward and upward to move into an inverted position. Block, or push off, the trapezoid vault with your arms extended, keeping your body straight. Continue rotating through in this position and land in demi-plié. Extend your legs and finish in a straight stand. Common errors in the handspring vault are letting your body get into a pike position or arching your back, or bending your arms when you make contact with the vaulting table.

7 UNEVEN BARS

Working on the uneven bars is one of the most exciting events in gymnastics, because it combines grace, power, and artistry. For young gymnasts, it is also a great test of strength. You will use your hands to grip the bar, your arms to pull you up, and your stomach muscles to lift your legs up when you swing and go around the bar. Your progress on the uneven bars will depend on your strength.

Just like the other gymnastics events, you will follow progressions to develop your skills. You will practice the basics on a bar that will be adjusted to the proper height to make it easy for you to grab the bar.

GRIPS

It is important to grip the bar properly. Hold the bar in your palms for a stronger and safer grip. That way, even if your fingers come off the bar, you'll still have some part of the hand holding it. Your school will have special chalk that you can use. Ask your instructor for advice on handgrips, which protect against blisters.

There are four ways you can hold onto the bar, although most of the time you will use the first two.

Overgrip: You will use this grip to get on the bar most of the time. Stand behind the bar. Put the back of your hands in front of you. Curl your fingers over the bar.

Mixed grip: You will use this grip to turn on the bar. Put one hand over the bar. Wrap the fingers of your other hand under the bar.

Protective handgrips

Overgrip

Under grip

Mixed grip

Undergrip: Wrap your fingers under the bar. You can see your fingers and palms.

Eagle grip: This grip is for much more advanced gymnasts. Spread out your thumbs, the way an eagle spreads its wings. It is also called the "dorsal grip."

HOW TO SWING

Learning how to swing properly will help you avoid injury and be able to perform your routines properly. Start by hanging onto the bar. Your instructor will give you a little push. Swing slow and steady, like the pendulum of a grandfather clock. Always let go only when you see the bar in front of you. If you let go with the bar behind you, you'll run the risk of falling backward and injuring yourself.

TAP SWING

Start your swing with the bar in front of you, moving forward. Your back should be curved forward and your feet slightly out in front of you, so that you form the shape of a banana or a C. This is the hollow-body position.

Pass through the bar (swing under the bar and past a vertical position). As your body moves ahead of your feet, arch your back to allow your feet to catch up. This is called the "arch position." Use your legs to "tap" up, or generate the power in your forward swing. The power of your tap determines the distance and speed of your swing. As you get used to the tap swing, you will learn how to generate more power and increase the height, or amplitude, of your swing.

Swing back to your starting position, and focus on regripping the bar when you reach the top of your backswing, as the momentum of your swing can pull your hands away from the bar. Knowing when to let go is an important skill when you perform the tap swing. Your goal should be to let go at the point on your forward or back swing when you are not moving up or down, but are "stalled" momentarily.

TAP SWING WITH A HALF TURN

This exercise is almost identical to the tap swing except that you swing through the tap so the bar is behind you, then switch to a mixed grip so that you can turn around. This can also be used as part of a dismount.

GLIDE SWING

Start in the hollow position with your hands in front of the bar. Swing down in a gliding motion so your toes nearly touch the ground. Pass the bar and move to a stretch position. Swing back to your start position.

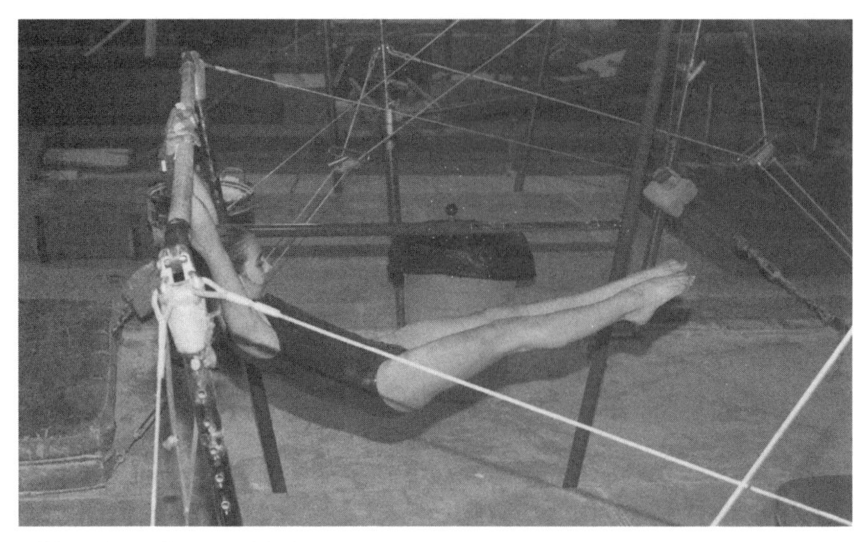

Glide swing (above and below)

PULLOVER

There's more to the uneven bars than just going back and forth, swinging. For instance, you'll practice standing on the low bar and moving onto the higher one; your instructor will adjust the bars so that you can easily reach the high bar.

The pullover, meanwhile, is like doing a backward roll over the bar. Start with a chin up. Pull your legs up and over the bar. Move the rest of your body around the bar while you regrip the bar with your palms. Hold the bar in front of your waist while keeping your arms and body straight. This is the front support position.

CAST

Put your hands on the bar in the overgrip position. Keep the weight on the heel of your hands. Look between your hands and focus on the bar. Keep your eyes on the bar throughout the move so that you are always

Cast (above and below)

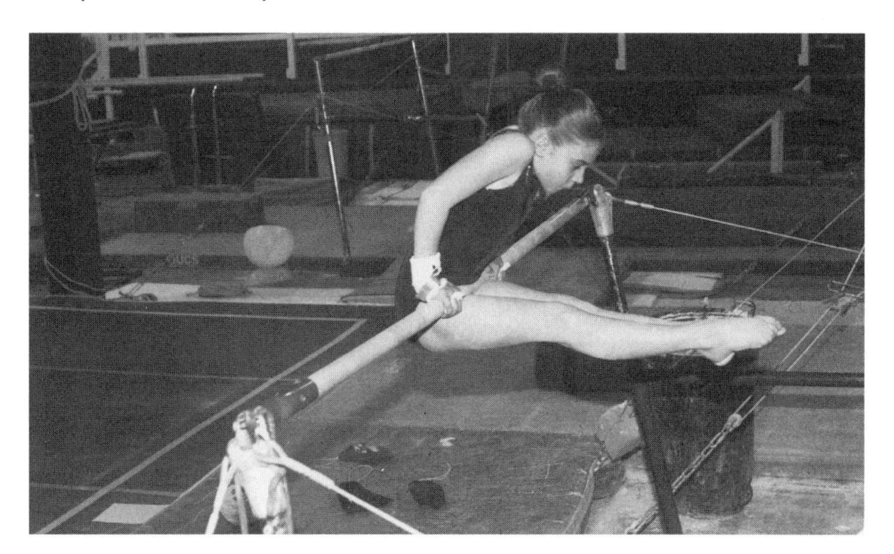

aware of your body position. Pull yourself up so that your waist touches the bar in the front support position. Push your hips away from the bar so that your back is curved forward and your feet are in front of you. Return to the bar in the front support position.

This is a cast up to a hollow-body position. Your shoulders are above the bar, and your stomach faces the ground.

BACK HIP CIRCLE

The back hip circle is a combination of the cast and pullover. If you can't do a pullover, you're probably not strong enough to do a back hip circle. You have to be able to keep your body straight and right next to the bar in order to circle around the bar. The bar is the center of the circle, and you use your body to revolve around it.

Start in the front support position, with your arms and body straight and the bar in front of your waist. Push your hips away from the bar to a hollow-body position and swing back to the bar. Drop your shoulders, place your hips against the bar, tuck in your chin, and go around the bar to return to the front support position.

SINGLE-LEG CUT

From the front support position, shift your weight to your left arm and swing your right leg, which should still be extended, over the bar. As you swing your leg over the bar, release your right hand for a moment and quickly regrasp the bar outside your right leg. Finish in a stride support using an overgrip, keeping your arms and legs straight.

FORWARD STRIDE CIRCLE

From a stride sit on the bar, change both of your hands to an undergrip and press down on the bar to lift your body off the bar in a stride support position. Extend your right leg forward with your left thigh touching the bar, and rotate forward, keeping your arms and upper body straight. Finish the circle where you started, in a clear stride support with your hands on top of the bar.

DISMOUNTS

Pike Sole-Circle Dismount

Execute a cast by swinging your legs forward, then backward and upward. Lift your body off the bar by pushing down against the bar

Pike sole-circle dismount (above and below)

with your hands, keeping your arms straight. With the balls of your feet on the bar between your hands and your legs in a tuck position, shift your shoulders back over the bar.

To dismount, straighten your legs and pull the bar against the bottoms of your feet. Swing backward and downward, then upward, keeping your feet pressed to the bar and your arms straight. As your hips rise on the upswing, release your feet from the bar and begin to extend your body as you press the bar backward with your hands. Release your hands and maintain a tight body position in midair. Land in demi-plié, and extend your arms and legs to finish in a straight stand.

Underswing Dismount

Press the bar downward with your hands in an overgrip so that the bar is at mid- to lower thigh level. Your arms should be straight. Stay in this position as you lean your shoulders backward and circle the bar with your hips away from the bar. As your hips rise, open the shoulder angle and press the bar backward. Keep a straight hollow-body position with your arms and legs straight throughout the motion. Release your hands and dismount in an extended position, keeping a tight body position in midair. Land in demi-plié and extend your arms and legs to finish in a straight stand.

8
BALANCE BEAM

The balance beam raises the challenge and grace of floor exercises to a higher level. You can practice on the floor all of the skills that you use on the balance beam, and before you progress to the low and high beam, you will first practice a straight line on the floor. When you have mastered this first skill, you will move to the beam. Then you will learn how to walk, tiptoe, turn, jump, and do basic tumbling on this four-inch-wide piece of wood.

You will start on a low balance beam that sits right on the floor and can be adjusted. Other beams are higher and can also be adjusted to competitive levels about four feet above the floor. For your confidence and safety, most schools have pads that fit over the beam. Plus, there will be plenty of mats underneath.

In one sense you must learn how to walk again when you start practicing on the balance beam. At first, you may feel unsteady and may fall off the beam. Don't be concerned—everyone goes through this. In time you will walk tall without a worry.

You begin with small steps, walking forward, backward, and sideways. You will practice all of these walks raised on your toes. This is the relevé position. Here is how you will walk on the beam.

WALK FORWARD

Stand straight with your chin up. Stretch your arms out to your sides to help keep your balance. Step along the beam in relevé. Try not to look down on the ground, although it will probably be hard not to at first.

Walking forward (above, right, and below)

WALK BACKWARD

Feel the beam with your feet. Take a step back in relevé, then feel again, then step, until you've reached the end of the beam. You won't be able to see where you are going, so it is important to feel the beam. You'll be tempted to shuffle your feet, but your instructor will remind you to step backward. At first, your instructor will be your guide. As you progress, your sense of where you are—your "spatial awareness"—will improve, as will your balance.

WALK SIDEWAYS

Keep your head and body straight and your arms out to the sides for balance.

Grapevine walk (this page and top of next page)

Take your first step to the side. Move your other foot next to it. Continue walking this way until you reach the end of the beam.

GRAPEVINE WALK

Face sideways on the beam. Cross one foot in front of the other as you move along the beam. Walk in the other direction by crossing one foot behind the other.

TURNS

As you find your footing on the beam, you will become more comfortable and graceful. It is important to know how to walk on your toes before you try these turns.

Pivot Turn

Stand flatfooted on the beam with your feet apart, which makes it easier to keep your balance. Raise onto your toes, in the relevé position, and pivot on the balls of your feet so that you face the other end of the beam. With practice, you will do this with your feet closer together. Eventually, your feet will be touching, which is the desired starting stance.

Squat Turn

Bend down into the squat position on the beam, with one foot in front of the other. Rise on the balls of your feet and turn around on the beam.

Squat turn (above and top of next page)

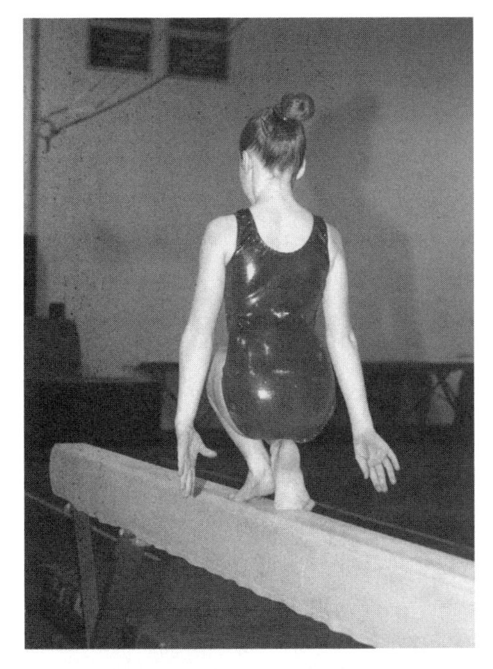

Forward kick turn (above and next page)

Forward Kick Turn

Stand on the beam. More your arms to the side for balance. Kick one leg in front of you and do a small hop and pivot with your other foot so you are facing the other direction.

PASSÉ

Stand on the beam. Move your arms out to the side for balance. Lift one of your feet and bring your big toe to your other knee, which is called the "passé position." Kick your bent leg out to step back onto the beam. Practice this skill with your feet flat and on your toes in relevé.

COUPÉ

Stand on the beam. Move your arms straight out to the side for balance.

Pointing your right foot forward, step forward by pushing off your left foot while reaching forward with your right leg onto the right foot in a relevé to flat motion. As your weight transfers to your right foot, point your left foot behind you, then bend your left knee forward and, while pointing your left foot, bring your left foot forward and down to touch your right ankle. Repeat the walk on your left leg.

DIP WALK

Stand on the beam. Move your arms out to the side for balance. Bend one knee and dip your opposite foot next to the beam. Place your foot back onto the beam as you straighten your knee. You can dip walk forward and backward.

LUNGE WALK

Stand on the beam and stretch your arms out to the side for balance. Step forward, and bend your front leg while lowering your other knee to the beam. Stand up and lunge forward with your back foot. Repeat these lunge steps to move along the beam.

LEG SWING IN RELEVÉ

Step forward with your left leg, keeping the foot flat on the beam. Swing your right leg forward and upward until it is parallel to the beam while raising your left foot to relevé. Bring your right leg down so that your right foot is in front of the left foot in relevé, with the heel of the right foot pressed against the front of the left foot. Pause, and repeat with the left leg swinging this time.

ARABESQUE (FRONT SCALE)

Stand on the beam. Move your arms out to the side for balance. Lift the back leg to at least the height of your front knee. Lean forward with your upper body as you lift your back leg further up. Keep both legs straight.

KNEE SCALE

Stand on the beam. Step forward. Lower your back knee on the beam. Place your hands in front of you on the beam to support yourself. Move your front leg behind you and lift it up so that it is straight.

Knee scale

V sit

V SIT

Sit on the beam. Put your hands behind your hips on the beam for support. Lift your legs into a V position.

FORWARD ROLL

Start with a forward roll on the floor beam. Move up to a higher beam with a fitted pad and a spotter for safety. There isn't much danger, because by this point everyone knows how to roll properly, and the floor will be padded with thick mats.

Step forward with your right foot in relevé and press the heel of your left foot, in relevé, behind the right foot. Lower to a tuck stand, reach forward, and put both hands on the beam. Tuck your chin to your chest and keep your back rounded. Lift your hips and place the back of your head and shoulders on the beam between your hands and feet. Push off both feet and start the roll, extending your legs into a pike position.

As you come out of the roll, tuck your legs and step out first with your left foot, then your right until you are in a tuck stand. Straighten both legs and finish with your right leg straight, your left leg extended behind at a 30-degree angle, and your left foot pointed downward.

One-knee mount

Front-on mount

MOUNTS

One-Knee Mount

Lift one knee onto the beam and stand up. Use your hands and arms to support yourself.

Front-on Mount

Put your hands on the beam. Push up so that your thighs are resting between your hands. Use your hands to stand up.

Step-up Mount

Run to the beam at an angle. Step onto the beam with your front leg. Put your hand on the beam for support.

Squat-on Mount

Run to the beam and jump off the springboard. Land with your knees bent and your feet together so that you're squatting. Stand up to start the rest of your routine.

DISMOUNTS

Several jumps that you practiced on the floor are used on the beam and to get off, or dismount. Start all of these jumps with your feet spread apart. As mentioned earlier, it is important to absorb the impact by landing on the balls of your feet with your knees bent. You can dismount at the side of the beam or on either end.

Squat-on mount

Ninety-Degree Turn to Straight Jump Dismount

This is the most basic of dismounts. With hands on hips and both feet in relevé, turn to face the side of the beam. In demi-plié, jump off the beam, extending your arms overhead and

Ninety-degree turn to tuck dismount (above, right, and next page)

keeping your body extended. Land in demi-plié, and extend your arms and legs to finish in a straight stand.

Ninety-Degree Turn to Tuck Jump Dismount

With arms lifted to the height of your head and both feet in relevé, turn sideways on the beam. Raise your arms to high position, demi-plié, and jump off the beam in a tuck position with your knees bent a minimum of 90 degrees and your thighs parallel to the floor. Before the landing, quickly extend your hips and legs, and land in demi-plié. Extend your arms and legs to finish in a straight stand.

Cartwheel to Side Handstand Dismount

Step forward onto your left leg, keeping it straight. Lift the right leg, keeping it straight, to 90 degrees or higher. Bring your right leg down and take a long step onto the ball of your right foot and lift your left leg upward and backward. Lower your right heel so your foot is flat on the beam.

Lower your torso and lift your left leg backward and upward, and reach forward and place your right hand sideways on the beam as you turn your body 90 degrees. Put your left hand on the beam sideways, keeping your hands shoulder-width apart as your right leg pushes off the beam into a side handstand with your legs together. Hold for one second, then lower your body to land in demi-plié, facing the beam. Finish in a straight stand.

TRAMPOLINE

The trampoline is more than just a plaything. It is a tremendous teaching tool and can help improve your jumping. Before you try the trampoline, however, you have to know how to land safely and follow a few rules.

- Practice the safety stop landing on the floor first. Land feet first, with your knees bent and your arms extended facing downward. Never jump or try to land on your head.
- One at a time on the trampoline. No exceptions. You risk injury when two or more people jump.
- Wait to be watched. Make sure you are being supervised.
- Always jump in the middle of the trampoline. The springs along the edges can throw you sideways where there aren't mats.
- Do not bounce out of control. Injuries occur when you rebound off the trampoline. More forceful bouncing means that you have to absorb more shock, which increases your risk of a serious injury.

The trampoline was built for jumping, so you'll spend most of your time improving moves you learned on the floor. Use your arms and legs to jump into the stretched position, which is used in many jumps. You will also practice straddle jumps, star jumps (your arms and legs are spread apart to form a star), tuck jumps, pike jumps, jumps with half turns, and jumps with full turns. There's also the split jump, with one leg in front of you and the other behind you.

Safety stop landing

MINI-TRAMPOLINE

The mini-trampoline, or trampette, is very similar to the vault. You will jump higher off the trampette, so it's exciting and fun. Unlike the spring-

Straddle jump

Star jump

Tuck jump

Pike jump

board, you don't have to worry about jumping off the right spot. You will get in the air, so the trampette is a good training device for the vault and floor exercises. It takes a few jumps to get comfortable with the mini-tramp. Then you combine an approach run with jumps from the stretch, straddle, tuck, pike, half-turn, and full-turn positions.

The height of your jumps makes it easier to do handstands and flips. Run onto the trampette. Jump high enough to launch yourself into a handstand. Fall flat on the mat. You've done what's called a handstand flat back.

You can also run and jump from the trampette into a forward roll. With practice, you will increase the height, or amplitude, of your jump and eventually you'll be able to do a front flip.

Then you can do a front handspring. Run onto the trampette and jump onto the padded block. Spring into a handstand to land on your feet.

Your instructor will turn the trampette around so that you can practice jumps backward. Finally, you may have stick contests, where the object is to land without moving your feet.

9 COMPETING IN GYMNASTICS

As you begin to acquire gymnastic skills, you may want to start testing your abilities against those of other gymnasts. This can take the form of in-house competitions held at your gym or outside competitions in your area, state, or even across the country. You cannot compete in USA Gymnastics–sponsored competitions until you are seven years old.

The USA Gymnastics Women's Junior Olympic Program consists of 10 levels. To prepare mentally and physically for increasingly higher-level competition takes time and patience. You must pass through a series of tests to make sure you are ready to compete safely and successfully.

Levels 1–4 prepare the gymnast for more intense and demanding events, so before you can participate in the Junior Olympic Program, you must be able to meet the Pre–Level 1 Conditioning and Flexibility requirements. Having done that, you must satisfactorily complete 75 percent of the routine requirements.

Each exercise consists of 12 points on which a gymnast is evaluated (with the exception of the vault). A gymnast must successfully complete nine of the 12 points in order to pass. In vaulting, there are four points per skill, and the gymnast must successfully complete three out of the four points in order to pass.

To meet the Conditioning and Flexibility requirements, five out of the six conditioning exercises at each level must be completed, and all events must be successfully completed. Gymnasts may progress and move through the levels at their own rate on individual events, but to advance to Level 5, all events at Levels 1–4 must be completed.

Levels 5 and 6 athletes can now complete at local, sectional, and state competitions. Level 7 combines compulsory required elements with optional choreography; this level is designed to bridge the gap between compulsory and optional gymnastics. Requiring gymnasts to perform specific "core" elements ensures that each athlete is capable of performing the elements that provide the basis for "optional" gymnastics. The gymnast is given creative freedom in the order of performance of the required elements, as well as the choreography that connects them.

Level 8 is the first level in which the gymnast must develop an individual optional exercise in each of the four events. At this point, judges look more for good execution and presentation than at the difficulty of each element. Competition is conducted at local, sectional, state, and regional levels.

At Levels 9 and 10, a gymnast can become an Intermediate or Advanced Junior Olympic athlete. Local, sectional, state, and regional championships are held and culminate in the East/West Championships for Level 9 and the National Championships for Level 10.

TIPS ON COMPETING

Performing in competition in front of judges and spectators is very different from doing routines on your own with only your instructor and classmates watching. One way to block out the distractions and keep your mind focused on your routine is to familiarize yourself with each part of the gym that you will be using during the competition, especially if it is a gym you have never visited before.

Make sure you know where everything is—apparatus, benches, spectators, judges' table—in the gym, and use your warm-up to get used to the surroundings. Are there any potential distractions near any of the apparatus? Are spectators close to the mats or far away? Is the sound system so loud that you can't hear yourself think? Is the equipment in good condition? There is an infinite number of small things that can get your mind off what you have to do, so try to anticipate as many of them as possible.

Mental imagery is very important as well. If you are doing a floor routine, stand where you're going to be doing it so you know what you're going to be looking at when you reach a certain point in the routine. This will help you keep your bearings.

VISUALIZATION

Visualization is a technique that has become increasingly popular with elite and professional athletes over the last several years. It is based on the idea that the brain processes something we have vividly imagined in much the same way it processes something that actually happened. In other words, if you vividly imagine yourself gliding effortlessly through your floor exercise routine, then your brain and nervous system will treat it as though it has actually happened, which will make you better prepared to turn the vision into reality.

This is not to say that you should stop practicing your routine. On the contrary, visualization will work only if you combine it with your regular workouts. But many athletes have found that they can more accurately re-create the physical conditions of a match in their mind than they could during a typical practice session.

HOW DO I DO IT?

To start with, you need to remember that visualization is something that will take practice to develop. You may also need to adjust your physical surroundings to create a relaxed environment in which there are no distractions. You can do this anywhere, as long as you can put yourself in a calm, relaxed state in order to "clear the decks" in your mind of any outside thoughts and concentrate on visualizing.

There are two methods used in visualization. One is to picture yourself doing the motions so that you are experiencing the sensations firsthand. This is called "subjective visualization." The other is to "watch" yourself in the second person, which is called "objective visualization." This is like watching a videotape of yourself. Subjective visualization is effective for focusing on the physical skills you will need in a match, while objective visualization may help you more with intangibles such as how you will react in certain situations.

Here are some guidelines to follow when you are visualizing.

- Practice your visualization regularly; try to spend some time on it every day, no matter if it is only five or 10 minutes. The important thing is to be consistent.
- Be detailed with your visualizations, and use all your senses. This will enhance the effects of the images.
- Pinpoint any specific skills that have been giving you trouble and visualize practicing them. This will help you when you are actually on the apparatus practicing.
- If you have access to video images of yourself doing gymnastics, use these to aid your visualization.

STAYING MOTIVATED

As you get older and develop more interests, it is not always easy to maintain your enthusiasm for some activities. This can happen frequently with young athletes who start competing at an early age. You may feel that you are not improving at the rate you would like to, or that you are not performing the way you should be. At these times, it is easy to question whether all the effort you are putting in is worth it.

Whether you compete at a high level in gymnastics or are just starting out, motivation is going to be the driving force behind any forward strides you make as an athlete. It helps you deal with frustration, tackle difficult situations, maintain a practice routine, and handle pressure.

There are many reasons an athlete loses motivation. It could be related to pressures you put on yourself or pressures that come from your parents or coaches. Or, you might feel you aren't getting better fast enough. Sometimes you have to stop and figure out why you are doing a particular activity such as gymnastics: Because it's fun? Because your friends do it? Because you want to be in the Olympics? Because your parents want you to do it? When things aren't going the way you want them to, sometimes it can help to ask yourself these questions.

DEFINING SUCCESS

Success is the solution to most motivation problems. This sounds surprisingly simple, but there is more to it than meets the eye. It all comes down to how you define success and making sure your definition is a realistic one that won't set the bar too high or too low.

In sports and in society in general, "second place is for losers" unfortunately seems to have become the prevailing idea. If you don't "win the big one," people seem to believe, it does not matter that you won all the matches or games to reach the big one while all the other athletes or teams except one have been eliminated. This is ridiculous, of course, unless you are one of the top athletes in the world. The rest of us need to measure success in terms other than just wins and losses, though naturally these will factor into the equation.

Try not to view success as just another word for finishing first. It should instead be tied in with giving your best effort, improving your technique, or any number of other things. Achieving success requires setting goals for yourself. These are basically challenges you set for yourself, and they can be big or small, short term or long term. They can be as modest as adding a new twist to your floor exercise routine or as ambitious as earning a gymnastics scholarship to college. The key is to understand the relationship between performance goals, which focus on measurements like improving your skills and technique, and outcome goals, which focus on the end result—wins and losses.

10
Rhythmic Gymnastics

Rhythmic gymnastics is a sport that combines dance and gymnastics with the use of balls, hoops, ribbons, ropes, and clubs. Gymnasts perform on a carpet to music; in competition, they perform leaps, pivots, balances, and other elements to demonstrate flexibility and coordination. The apparatus is fully integrated into the routine, and specific moves are performed with each apparatus.

Unlike in regular floor exercise, acrobatic skill is not allowed in rhythmic gymnastics, and a rhythmic gymnast would be penalized for using it. Pre-acrobatic elements such as backward and forward shoulder rolls are permitted, as are walkovers and cartwheels. Originality and risk are important parts of the sport, and every routine is different.

Having originated in Scandinavia, rhythmic gymnastics remains primarily a European sport for women and girls. A small percentage of American gymnasts choose rhythmic gymnastics, which means that in the United States there is not as much competition in rhythmic gymnastics as there is in conventional gymnastics.

Competition is divided into two sections:

- Rhythmics consist of group exercises with natural and harmonic elements carried out to music. It develops among a "team" coordination, flexibility, strength, and balance through movements that are reciprocal, alternating between contraction and relaxation. It emphasizes fluidity and connections between moves so that in lifting the arm, for example, the movement travels from the center of the body all the way out to the fingertips.
- Competitive (which did not develop until the 1960s) consists of individual exercises, for which gymnasts are judged on technical

merit, expression, and composition. The gymnast must perform certain compulsory elements as well as optional original elements that can add bonus points for creativity.

APPARATUS

A rhythmic gymnast learns to work and coordinate body movements with the following "props."

Ball: Made of rubber or plastic, the ball can be 18 centimeters to 20 centimeters in diameter. It must weigh at least 400 grams. It can be any color, including gold and silver. The ball is the only apparatus for which no grip is allowed, demanding a more harmonious, unbroken relationship with the body. Gymnasts perform many movements with the ball involving rolling, bouncing, or tossing. They may toss the ball in the air, do two forward rolls and then catch it, or they may roll the ball or bounce it off a body part.

Hoop: Made of wood or plastic, the hoop must be of rigid nonbending material. It must be 80 to 90 centimeters wide on the inside. It can be rough or smooth and can be wholly or partially wrapped with same or different-colored adhesive tape. The color is optional, including gold and silver. The gymnast moves within the space provided by the hoop, requiring frequent changes of grip. Judges look for smoothly coordinated movements; the hoop's shape favors rolls, passages, rotations, and walkovers.

Clubs: They can be wood or plastic and must be 40 to 50 centimeters in length. Each must weigh at least 150 grams, and the head's diameter is a maximum of three centimeters. Clubs are bottle shaped and consist of three parts: the body (bulbous), the neck (slim part), and the head (spherical). The three parts can be wrapped with an adhesive or nonslip tape. They can be any single color or combination of colors. The gymnast uses them to execute rolls, twists, and as many asymmetric figures as possible. Exercises using clubs require a highly developed sense of rhythm, hand-eye coordination, and precision.

Rope: It can be made of hemp or any synthetic material. The length must be proportionate to the gymnast's height. It has knots at the ends, not handles. The ends can be wrapped to a length of 10 centimeters. It can be any color. Technical figures are made with the rope taut or loose, with one or both hands, and with or without change of hands. The relationship with the gymnast is more dynamic and exciting than with the other apparatus: The rope often appears as a serpentlike attacker, seizing and winding around the gymnast. Judges look for suppleness, agility, and elegance.

Ribbon: Made of satin or an unstarched derivative, the ribbon is four to six centimeters wide and at least six meters long in one piece. It must weigh at least 35 grams without the stick and attachment. It can be any color. The ribbon's stick can be made of wood, plastic, or fiberglass. It can be a maximum of one centimeter in diameter and must be 50 to 60 centimeters in length, including the attachment ring. It is cylindrical or conical or a combination of both, and can be any color. The ribbon's attachment may be of any suitable material. The ribbon is long and light and may be thrown in all directions. Its function is to create designs in space, and its flight through the air make images and shapes of every kind. Snakes, spirals, and throws are essential moves.

ROUTINES

An individual routine is performed by one gymnast with one apparatus for one to one and a half minutes; a group routine is performed by six gymnasts with six pieces of apparatus for two and a half to three minutes. Both are accompanied by music, often a piano. There are no compulsory elements at the elite and international levels in rhythmic gymnastics. Artistry—including originality of a routine and its executions, gestures and facial expressions, and fluidity of line and movement—counts far more than vigorous acrobatics in scoring points.

STUDYING RHYTHMIC GYMNASTICS

You can start studying rhythmic gymnastics as early as five or six years old. You will begin with very basic skills and build from there. Rhythmic gymnastics is heavily based on the vocabulary, movements, and physical demands of ballet, so if you have studied ballet already you will be ahead of the game when you start rhythmic gymnastics. If not, don't worry. You will learn many of the same movements and vocabulary, such as jeté (leap), grand battement (high kick), tendue (stretched foot with pointed toe), relevé (rising up on the toes), and plié (deep knee bend with knees out to the side). Tumbling skills are not crucial, as you will learn them as you progress. These will be skills such as front and back walkovers, cartwheels, and one-handed cartwheels.

As in ballet, it is important to have a certain body type because the lines made by your arms and legs must be clean and beautiful. Girls with long legs and long arms are best suited. A short torso is fine, and a lean figure is desirable. As with ballet, in which dancers turn out their legs from the hips so that they put their ankle first when pointing their foot, the ability to rotate easily at the hip is essential. Strong feet with high arches are also helpful for the line they create when posing. Strength is not important, but flexibility is; rhythmic gymnastics involves much bending, twisting, spinning, and stretching.

Speed is also important when you are performing floor routines. As in ballet, rhythmic gymnastics builds skills slowly until you are doing a three-hour class. It starts with a typical ballet class of one hour at the barre, which is a wooden rail where you do exercises and stretches; then another half hour of free movement in the center of the room. Only after your muscles have been warmed and loosened, and your technique perfected, will you move into a rhythmic gymnastics class for another hour and a half. When you are starting out in rhythmic gymnastics, you will be given an apparatus to work with, such as the hoop or ball, and you will learn rolls, throws, spins, and other simple movements.

RHYTHMIC GYMNASTICS TIME LINE

Rhythmic gymnastics grew out of the Swedish system of free exercise developed in 1814 by Per Henrik Ling. Ling promoted aesthetic gymnastics in which students expressed their feelings and emotions through bodily movement. The idea was extended by an American woman, Catherine E. Beecher, founder of the Western Female Institute in Ohio in 1837. In Beecher's gymnastics program, young women exercised to music, moving from simple calisthenics to more strenuous activities.

Some other important moments in the development of rhythmic gymnastics are listed below.

1930s: The ball becomes an important centerpiece of rhythmic gymnastics, used while the athlete runs, walks, and swings. The rope is first used in the 1930s by a Swedish group, and the hoop becomes popular after a demonstration in the 1936 Olympic Games.

1945: Rhythmic gymnastics is accepted as a sport in the Soviet Union; Russian rhythmic gymnastics heavily emphasizes back flexibility and the movements found in classical ballet.

1949: The first rhythmic gymnastics national championships are held in the Soviet Union.

1951: Fédération Internationale de Gymnastique (FIG), the international governing body for gymnastics, establishes the term *modern gymnastics.*

1954: The rope, hoop, ball, and ribbon become the prescribed apparatus, and rules are established to standardize floor exercises. At this point the sport is still purely for recreation or performance and not for competition.

1960s: The first program for competitive rhythmic sportive gymnastics is started in the 1960s in California by Alla Svirsky.

1961: The first international competition is held between the Soviet, Bulgarian, and Czech delegations and is dominated by the Soviets.

1962: The FIG recognizes rhythmic gymnastics as a sport.

1963: The first world championships are held in Budapest, and 28 athletes from 10 European countries compete. At that first event, the competition consists of only two routines—one a free routine and one with a choice of rope, hoop, or ball (clubs and ribbons were not used until later).

1971: Rhythmic gymnastics becomes a full four-apparatus event. The ribbon is compulsory, and rope, ball, and hoop are freestyle.

1973: Clubs become compulsory, and the hoop, ball, and ribbon are freestyle, marking the start of the custom of selecting four of the five apparatus with which to compete. The United States sends its first rhythmic gymnastics delegation to the Rhythmic World Championships. The name *modern rhythmic gymnastics* is coined.

1984: Rhythmic Gymnastics Individual competition is introduced as an Olympic discipline. LA Lights, one of the most prestigious international meets, begins in Culver City, California.

1987: Bulgarian gymnast Bianka Panova makes it into the *Guinness Book of World Records* with a perfect performance of 10.0 in all eight routines. She wins five gold medals at the world championship in Varna, Bulgaria.

1988: The first perfect score of 10 is recorded at the Seoul Olympics.

1996: Rhythmic Gymnastics Group competition is added to the Olympics, and the Spanish take the gold medal. The apparatus is five hoops, three balls, and two ribbons. For the first and only time, an Olympic commemorative medal is struck for rhythmic gymnastics.

1997: The Code of Points, used for scoring, is changed to place greater emphasis on body techniques; execution now counts for 50 percent of the total score. Cartwheels and other acrobatics are now allowed.

11
CHEERLEADING

Cheerleading requires a combination of athleticism, dance, and gymnastics. It incorporates such elements of dance as grace, timing, and strength with the balance, flexibility, skills, speed, and daring of gymnastics. Unlike either of those disciplines, cheerleading also requires dedicated teamwork, as you must synchronize a routine with a squad that can number from a few people to as many as 40.

Like dancers, cheerleaders memorize many different dance routines, and like gymnasts, they fly through the air, tumble, and twist—and rely on the skill and attention of their spotters and teammates to help them land safely. Whether you consider it a sport, an art, or a discipline, cheerleading calls for endurance, extreme flexibility, and the ability to perform well no matter what the circumstances.

Cheerleading today blends entertainment and student leadership and affects people at many levels. Individually, the cheerleader develops athletic skills, leadership, and teamwork; the team builds school spirit, and the school's spirit and ability to attract attendance at school games helps build community spirit. It all starts with you!

HISTORY

Cheerleading originated at Princeton University, in New Jersey, in the 1870s, when at a football game, Thomas Peebler gathered six men to lead a yell on the sidelines. In 1883 Peebler brought the custom to the University of Minnesota, and there, on November 2, 1898, a cheerleader named Johnny Campbell got so excited that he jumped out in front of the crowd—and a new sport was born. The University of Minnesota is also credited with creating the first school "fight song."

Women became active in cheerleading in the 1920s. In the 1930s, pom-pom routines were introduced using paper poms, still the most popular cheerleading prop. When men went to war in 1940s, women became more involved in the sport, and in 1948 Lawrence Hurkimer, founder of the spirit industry, organized the first cheerleader camp at Sam Houston University, in Texas, with 52 girls in attendance. The first cheerleading organization, the National Cheerleading Association, was founded that same year.

Cheerleading was first shown on national television in 1978, when CBS broadcast the Collegiate Cheerleading Championships. In 1976 the Dallas Cowboy Cheerleaders performed at Super Bowl X, which started a trend of "dancing cheerleaders." The 1970s also marked the beginning of high school and collegiate cheerleading competitions.

Some celebrities who are former cheerleaders include Paula Abdul, Halle Berry, Katie Couric, Susan Lucci, and Madonna.

Following are some standard cheerleading moves.

TUMBLING

Roundoff Back Handspring

Roundoff back handspring (above and top of next page)

This is a combination of two basic tumbling moves. The first stage of the combination is the roundoff followed by a backward handspring. For the roundoff, take a long step forward into a right lunge, with your right leg slightly or halfway bent. Place your right hand on the floor with the fingers pointing to the right as your body turns 90 degrees left. Place your left hand on the floor with the fingers pointing toward your right hand. Both hands should be in a straight line directly in front of the right foot. Kick the left leg backward and upward overhead, passing through a brief sideward straddled handstand. After your feet are vertical turn 90

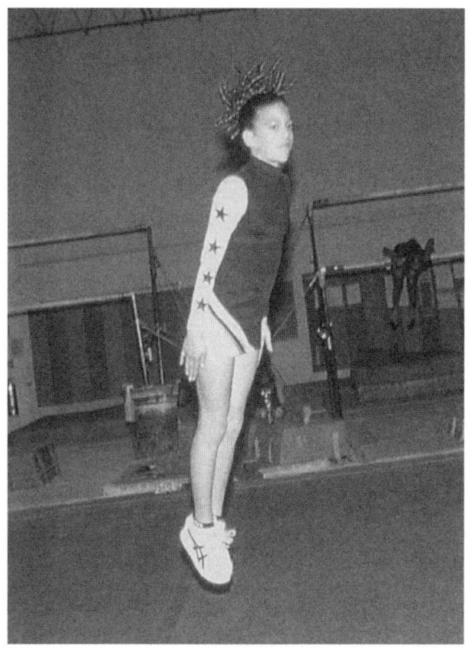

Roundoff back handspring tuck (above)

degrees left and join your legs. Push explosively off the floor with your arms and shoulders while snapping your legs down and under to land on both feet in an upright hollow, slightly curved body position. To complete the combination continue without pause into the handspring move. For the handspring, immediately push your body up and back overhead with both legs. Reach up and back with your arms. Continue to rotate backward and land in a balanced and controlled position. Then, add a dash of cheerleading flair by finishing with a slight jump.

Roundoff Back Handspring Tuck

This is a variation of the back handspring in which the legs are tucked during the body's backward rotation overhead. After pushing your body up and back overhead simply lift your knees toward your hands into a minimum of a 90-degree tuck position. Continue to rotate backward and finish in a balanced, controlled position and a slight jump.

Roundoff back handspring full layout

Roundoff Back Handspring Full Layout

This is another variation of the back handspring in which the legs are extended during the body's backward rotation overhead. After pushing your body up and back overhead extend your feet and legs. Continue to rotate backward and finish in a balanced, controlled position and slight jump.

Standing Tuck

Pause to visualize the movement you're about to make. Take a deep breath and focus. Raise your arms and join hands in front of the chin. Forcefully drop your arms to the sides and shift the weight to the balls of your feet. Thrust your hands and arms overhead and explosively push up and back with your legs. Tuck your knees to your chest and grab hold of them with your hands. Continue rotating in a tight spin. After your head passes under your knees, release them, and quickly extend the legs in prepa-

Standing tuck (above and next page)

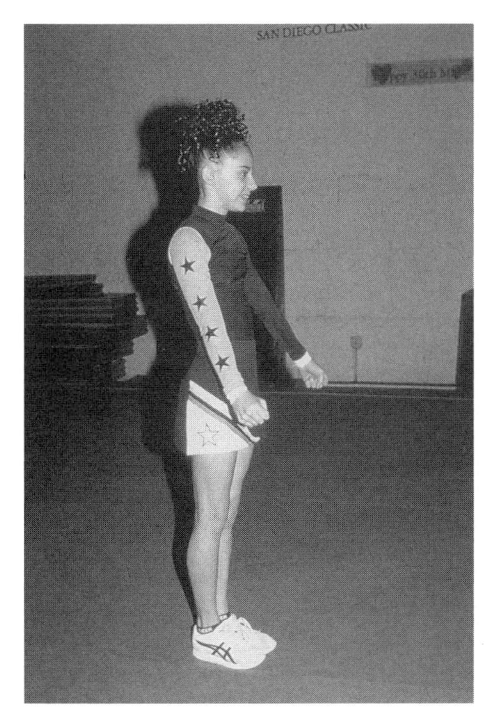

ration for the landing. Land in a controlled, balanced position—"stick" it if you can!

JUMPS

To be able to do the following jumps, it is important to practice daily, as well as to stay in good physical condition by doing other sports or aerobic exercises. Maintaining strength, flexibility, endurance, and general cardiovascular fitness will help you perform these jumps with confidence.

The best way to increase your height in these jumps is to do leg lifts with light (five-pound) weights and practice jumping for five minutes each day. Before long you'll feel yourself reaching new heights.

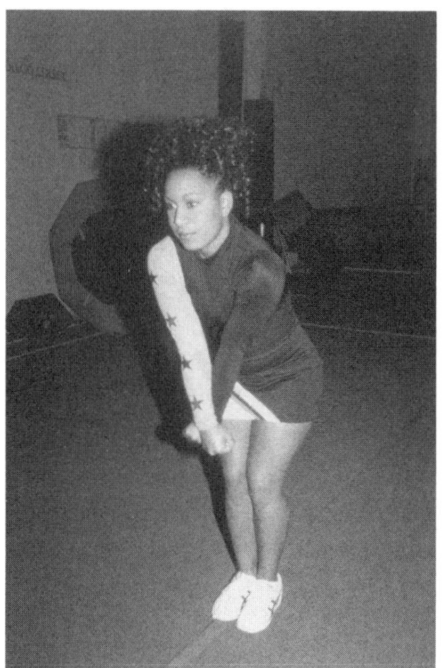

Pike jump (above, right, and bottom left)

Side hurdler (above and on next page)

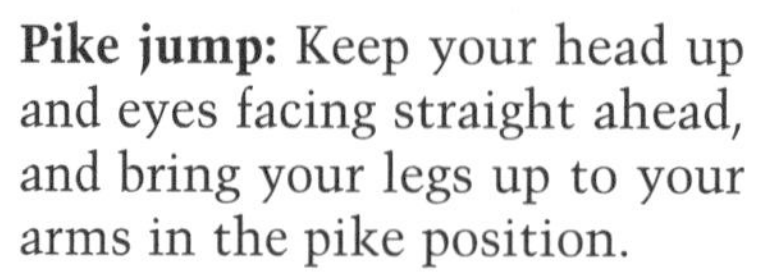

Pike jump: Keep your head up and eyes facing straight ahead, and bring your legs up to your arms in the pike position.

Side hurdler: Keep your bent knee facing the crowd as you extend the other leg in a hurdler position in the air.

Toe touch: Keep your head and chest up, pull your legs up to your outstretched arms, and reach for the arch of your foot.

STUNTS

Cheerleading stunts feature three positions: flyer, base, and spotter. The flyers perform the stunts in the air. The bases hold up the flyer or flyers and balance them high above the ground. The spotters help the flyers into the stunt, steady them, and catch them to prevent injury. The more spotters there are in a stunt, the safer it is for everyone, especially the flyers.

For advanced-level stunts, the building technique is as follows:

- Bases stand in a double lunge.
- One base grabs the flyer's heel and toe and holds her at waist level.

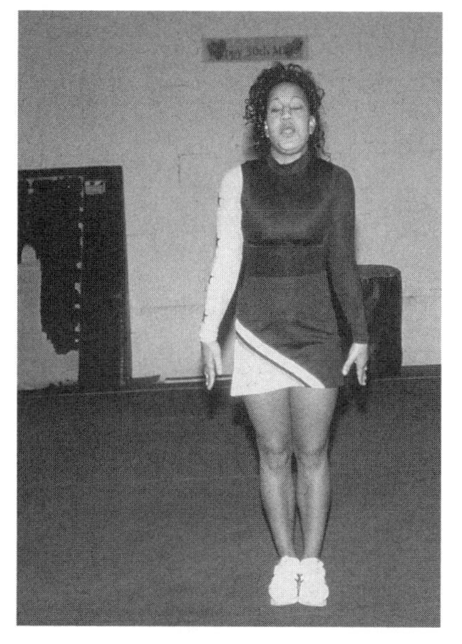

Toe touch (above, right, and below)

- The other base grabs the bottom of her foot with the inside hand.
- That base's outside hand is then wrapped on top of the foot with the thumb in the palm of the hand underneath.
- The third base (the "back spotter") grabs the flyer's ankle and places the other hand under the flyer's seat for a boost.
- The flyer then pushes off as the bases use their legs to push up the stunt.
- When the flyer hits the top, the bases lock their legs and complete the stunt.

Thigh stand (above, right, and bottom left)

Extension (above and top left of next page)

The Thigh Stand is an example of a basic cheerleading stunt. The Extension is a slightly more advanced stunt, and the Bow and Arrow, Heel Stretch, and Scorpion are considered advanced stunts.

Heel stretch (above)

Bow and arrow (above and top left of next page)

Scorpion (above)

THINGS TO REMEMBER DURING CHEERLEADING STUNTS

Bases: Always use legs to lift—never use your back.
Flyers: Weight should be on the shoulders of the bases when building.
Stay tight—squeeze your buttocks in.
Keep your head and chest up.
Spot the wall to keep focus.
Trust your bases.
Backspot: Catch from beginning to end.
Control the stunt.
Always keep your eyes on the flyer.

12
PARENTS AND TOTS

Parents are getting their kids involved in gymnastics earlier and earlier, it seems. It is not uncommon for 18-months-olds to begin attending classes once a week. As a parent, you can take an active role in introducing your child to gymnastics; in fact you are pretty much required to take an active role, but that's the fun part.

One important thing to keep in mind is that at this young age children can vary greatly in physical development and coordination. At 18 months, some kids can run, jump, hang and swing on a bar, and do all sorts of tumbling exercises. Others may need some coaxing to do these things or may not want to do them at all. What you'll probably find is that all toddlers, even the reluctant ones, quickly come to love the feeling of their bodies in motion, and then their development proceeds fairly rapidly.

Your gym will probably have you sign a standard liability release form before your youngster starts classes. When you first come in, the instructors will explain what to look out for, what areas not to go near, and which exercises should not be attempted without supervision. You'll also get a tour of the tumbling areas and apparatus, focusing on which surfaces are harder and which are softer so that you and your child will know what to expect as you change from one surface to another and won't get hurt. The tumbling floor mat, for example, is firm, and if you step from the tumbling floor onto the landing mat, which is the same height but softer, if you're not ready for it, you could trip and fall. Remember that safety has to do with using the correct technique as demonstrated by the instructor, and proceeding in a gradual progression, not jumping ahead.

The goals at this level of gymnastics are to develop coordination, balance, and body awareness. Your child will practice balancing on one foot, balancing on two feet, jumping on one foot or on two feet, and maintaining balance in the air, which is what the trampoline is used for. Doing these and other basic exercises will help your child develop leg strength, arm strength, and abdominal strength. Your instructor may also have your child explore equipment that will require her to go over, under, and through various obstacles.

Young children can use the trampoline right away and will work on doing a galloping motion to develop balance and seat drops to work on turning in midair. Depending on the progress of the child, handstands may come later. There is also a long, flat trampoline called a tumble track that is used for running and jumping.

Another fun piece of apparatus to use is the low balance beam, which is usually about six inches off the floor. Since there is little risk of injury at this low height—the beam is furthermore resting on mats—your instructor may encourage you to stay close to your child but not actually help her. This will help your child get used to balancing on her own.

Some parents will take their kids up to the regular-height beam and hold them or have the child hold their finger while they walk. This can be a significant challenge for a young child, so make sure your child is comfortable with being that high off the mat, and keep contact at all times. For babies, beam-walking is pretty much a challenge by itself. Have them go both ways, turn, and stand on one foot.

Many gyms are equipped with a rope and trapeze assembly that hangs over a foam pit. This gives kids an opportunity to swing in a controlled setting and learn how to judge the distance to the ground. They also learn how to jump off an object without worrying about the landing.

When your child reaches the age of two or three, she may start doing more actual gymnastics skills, such as handstands and cartwheels. Even younger kids can start with the handstand motion (up against a wall, for instance). The instructor will have them put their feet up against the wall while they are lying on the mat and gradually move their feet up the wall. This gets them used to supporting their weight with their arms over their heads, and as they get stronger they will gradually progress to doing the actual handstand.

Rolls are also an important part of learning gymnastics. Young children have to overcome the natural tendency to want to see where they're going at all times, and practicing forward rolls—and backward rolls, as they get a little more advanced—will help them achieve this. Eventually, the instructor will teach them how to do a backward roll and push into a handstand.

As your child becomes more advanced, she will get to practice pulling herself up and over on uneven parallel bars that are a lower version of the regular uneven bars. She'll do maneuvers like hanging from the bar in an inverted position, bringing her feet through her arms and putting her feet on the floor, a routine called Skin the Cat. These types of exercises help develop arm and shoulder strength.

Once your child reaches the age of three, she will probably work solely with the instructors and other kids in her class. While your direct involvement will end, you can take satisfaction in knowing that you have played an important role in introducing your child to a sport that will give her countless hours of enjoyment. She is now ready to start blossoming on her own, with your support and encouragement.

HOW TO BE A SUPPORTIVE PARENT

As the parent of a young athlete, it is crucial that you play a supportive role in your child's activities. This should be a relatively simple task, but for many adults it is not as easy as it sounds. Below are some guidelines.

1. **Focus on mastering skills and strategies rather than competitive ranking.** Sport mastery focuses on performance, which can be controlled by the athlete, while competitive ranking focuses primarily on winning and losing, an outcome that is frequently beyond the athlete's control. An overemphasis on competitive rank and an underemphasis on sport mastery are a primary cause of the dramatic dropout rate from competitive sports by 12- to 18-year-olds.
2. **Decrease the pressure to win.** Supportive parents realize that any sport creates its own pressure to succeed. Additional pressure from a parent is likely to be counterproductive, particularly in the long run. Supportive parents avoid making the outcome of a game larger than life. As a game or a competition becomes blown out of proportion, a youngster's self-esteem can become tied into winning or losing. A child should not feel less valuable or less loved when a match is lost.
3. **Believe that sport's primary value is the opportunity for self-development.** The probability of achieving lasting fame and glory via sports is low. Many outstanding athletes never achieve professional status, but their sports experiences have allowed them to develop lifelong values and self-respect.

(continues)

(continued)

4. **Understand the risks.** Competition places the athlete on center stage. Anytime you attempt to succeed publicly, you risk failing where others can judge you. In the long run competing is a willingness to risk failure. Giving your best is what athletics is all about.
5. **Communicate your true concerns directly with the coach.** A positive working relationship is based on clearly communicated, mutual goals among parents, coaches, and athletes. While a parent cannot control the behavior of a coach, he or she can communicate with the coach on a regular basis about the overall development of the child.
6. **Understand and respect the differences between parental roles and coaching roles.** Parents and coaches need to understand their different roles in supporting the young athlete. While parents are ultimately responsible for their child's development, once they have chosen a coach, they must leave the coaching to the coach. Even though supportive parents often play sports with their child, they avoid coaching "over the shoulder" of the coach or publicly questioning coaching decisions.
7. **Control negative emotions and think positively.** Few athletes wish to perform poorly. Negative reactions to poor performance only add to an athlete's pressures. Supportive parents realize that even the athlete who "chokes" is trying to succeed; in fact part of the problem with many athletes is that they are trying too hard to succeed. Criticizing does little to enhance performance.
8. **Avoid the use of fear.** The use of punishment and withdrawal of love can pressure kids to perform better. Unfortunately such strategies tend to trade short-term performance gains for long-term emotional risks to the youngster's health and well-being. Supportive parents recognize that a love for sport is rarely fostered by fear of the consequences of failure.
9. **Avoid criticizing.** Nagging parents often confuse support with constantly reminding the child that he or she needs to practice more, condition more, concentrate more, etc. Overly involved parents frequently lose their objectivity. They are unable to provide the critical emotional support children often need before and during highly competitive contests.

10. **Recognize and understand expressions of insecurity.** More often than not, youngsters who express high anxiety have parents who are insensitive to their symptoms. When children are nervous, uncertain, or feeling pressure, insensitive parents may trivialize the child's fear or see such concerns as signs of weakness. Supportive parents realize that such expressions are normal and are a call for emotional support.
11. **Avoid the use of guilt.** "We've done so much for you," or "The family's given up so much for you, the least you could do is to take advantage of what we've provided for you," are typical remarks of unsupportive parents. They use guilt to manipulate the child to perform the way the parents desire.
12. **Show empathy.** Empathy is an understanding of what the child is feeling and an awareness of the pressures and demands that the sport places on the athlete. Empathy is not necessarily sympathy or agreement but rather a true understanding that the task is difficult. A sympathetic response to an expression of doubt by the athlete might be, "Perhaps you're right. Perhaps it is too difficult. Maybe you shouldn't compete today." Empathy, on the other hand, might be expressed by a supportive parent as, "Yes, it will probably be a tough competition today. C'mon, let me help you get ready."

GLOSSARY

aerial A stunt in which the gymnast turns completely over in the air without touching the apparatus with his or her hands.

amplitude The height or degree of execution of a movement. In general, the higher or more breathtaking the movement, the better the amplitude—and the score.

apparatus One of the various pieces of equipment used in gymnastics training and competitions.

arabesque A basic standing position on one foot. The free leg is turned outward and held in the rear at a minimum of a 30-degree angle to the support leg.

arch position Stretching or bending in the upper and lower back.

assemblé A jump, taking off from one leg, swinging the other leg forward, and bringing the feet together before landing in a demi-plié.

balancé A walk of three dance steps with a demi-plié on the first step and relevé on the last two steps.

basic stand A standing position with the legs straight, together, torso erect, and head neutral.

candlestick A balance position high on the shoulders, with the hip angle open and body extended.

cast A swing movement on the bars that finishes in a clear support on the hands only.

chassé A walk consisting of a step and push off from one foot, closing the free foot in the air behind or next to the takeoff foot, landing on the opposite foot in demi-plié.

clear Describing a movement in which only the hands and not the rest of the body are in contact with the apparatus.

clear stride support On the uneven bars, one leg on each side of the bar (one leg forward, one leg backward). Hands support the body so that it remains off the bar.

composition The structure of a gymnastics routine. Each individual movement or skill is a building block; how they are arranged into an exercise is called the composition of the routine.

compulsories Predesigned routines that contain specific movements required of all gymnasts.

counterswing A backward swing on the bars.

coupé A position in which the leg is bent with the toe pointed on or behind the ankle, depending on the position of the support leg.

demi-plié Slight flexion of the knees, performed in all five positions of the feet and used in preparation for jumps, turns, and landings.

developé A movement of the leg whereby the leg initially bends with the toe touching the inside of the ankle of the support leg. From there the toe moves up the leg, then straightens to an extended finished position off the floor.

dismount To leave an apparatus at the end of a routine; usually done with a difficult twist or salto.

execution The performance of a routine. Form, style, and the technique used to complete the skills constitute the level of execution of an exercise. Bent knees, poor toe point, and an arched or loosely held body position are all examples of poor execution.

feet positions *First position:* Heels are touching with the toes turned out and perpendicular to the body. *Second position:* Feet are side by side approximately shoulder-width apart with the toes turned out and pointing away from the body. *Third position:* One foot is placed directly in front of the other and turned out with the heel off the front foot touching the middle of the other foot. *Fourth position:* Feet are placed one in front of the other, approximately 12–18 inches apart, with the toes turned out. The heel of the front foot should be directly in front of the big toe of the back foot. *Fifth position:* Feet are placed together one in front of the other with the toes turned out. *Fifth position relevé:* Same as fifth position but standing high on tiptoe with the heel of the front foot pressed against the front of the back foot.

flic-flac Also known as a flip-flop or back handspring. It consists of taking off from one or two feet, jumping backward onto the hands, and landing on the feet. This element is used in a majority of tumbling passes on the floor exercise. It's also used a great deal on the balance beam.

flip-flop See **flic-flac.**

flyaway A dismount from the uneven bar performed from a long swing to a finish with a salto.

forced arch A foot position on the balls of the feet with heels raised off the floor as high as possible.

front support A position on the bars or beam in which weight is balanced on hands with thighs resting on the apparatus.

giant A swing in which the body is fully extended and moving through a 360-degree rotation around the bar.

glide A forward swing on the low bar that finishes with the body extended.

handspring Springing off the hands by putting the weight on the arms and using a strong push from the shoulders; can be done either forward or backward. Usually the handspring serves as a linking movement.

hop A vertical jump on one foot.

hurdle A small skip step taken at the beginning of a stunt in order to gain speed on the run-up.

kip A movement from a position below the equipment to a position above.

layout position Straight or slightly arched body position that may be seen during a movement or a still position.

leap An overextended running step, taking off from one foot and landing on the opposite foot, with the legs split 90 to 180 degrees forward and backward.

lever A position used when moving into or out of a handstand in which the person stands on one foot and lifts the opposite leg in back with arms stretched overhead, creating a straight line from fingertips to toes.

lunge A movement to the front, back, or side in which front leg is flexed in demi-plié position and the opposite leg is extended.

mount The initial skill of a gymnastics routine.

opposition An arm position in which one arm is placed in a forward-middle position and the opposite arm is in side-middle.

optionals Personally designed routines that show the gymnast to the best advantage.

overgrip (regular grip) A hand position on the uneven bars in which the hands are placed on top of the bar with fingers forward and palms downward.

passé A leg position in which one leg is bent with the toe pointed against the inside of the knee of the support leg.

pike position A position in which the body is bent forward more than 90 degrees at the hips while legs are kept straight.

pirouette A changing of direction by twisting in the handstand position.

pivot turn A 180-degree turn performed in a stand high on the balls of the feet (relevé), which are pressed together.

plié A bending of the knees.

presentation Expressive, balletic movement in which arms open from forward-middle to a side-middle position.

release Leaving the bar to perform a move before regrasping it.

relevé Up on the ball of the foot.

routine A combination of stunts displaying a full range of skills on one apparatus.

salto A flip or somersault, with the feet coming up over the head and the body rotating around the axis of the waist.

scale A position used in floor exercise or balance beam in which the person stands on one foot and turns the free leg outward and lifts it behind to a minimum of a 90-degree angle to the support leg.

squared hips Both hips are flat and facing forward.

squat stand A position in which the knees and hips are flexed and the person supports him- or herself on the balls of the feet, which are close together. The torso is erect and the buttocks close to the heels but not touching them.

stick To show no movement of the feet upon landing.

straddle A position in which legs are extended sideward and turned outward and hips are extended.

straight hollow A position in which the body is straight, with hips flat, ribs down, chest in, and buttocks tight.

stride support A position on the bars in which a person's weight is balanced on the hands with one leg on either side of the bar.

tight arch Position in which arms are extended high overhead, the chest is lifted up and back, and hips are flat with the buttocks tight.

tuck A position in which the knees and hips are bent and drawn into the chest and the body is folded at the waist.

twist A rotation of the body around its longitudinal axis, defined by the spine. Not to be confused with a salto.

undergrip (reverse grip) A hand position on the uneven bars in which the hands are placed under the bar with fingers facing the body and palms upward.

virtuosity The artistry or the degree of rhythm and harmony displayed while a movement is executed. In general the more flowing and seamless a series of skills appears to be, the greater the virtuosity and the higher the score.

V sit Sitting in the pike position with trunk erect but leaning backward slightly and legs extended upward. Hips are supported from behind with the hands.

waltz step Three steps in a row: demi-plié through fourth position into relevé on the next two steps.

ASSOCIATIONS AND WEBSITES

American Gymnast
http://www.american-gymnast.com
3354 Sugar Mill Road
Augusta, GA 30907
Telephone: (877) 789-2267

American Internet Cheerleader Magazine
http://www.geocities.com/aicmzine

Cheerplace.com
http://www.cheerplace.com

Fédération International de Gymnastique
http://www.fig-gymnastics.com
Rue des Oeuches 10
Case Postale 359
2740 Moutier
Switzerland
E-mail: info@fig-gymnastics.org
Telephone: (41-32) 494-64-10
Fax: (41-32) 494-64-19

Gymmedia International
http://www.gymmedia.com
Herholz & Schmeißer GbR
PR-Agentur für Turnen, Gymnastik und Sport
Brachliner Straße 8
Berlin 12 683
Germany
E-mail: gymmedia.h@t-online.de

Telephone: (49-30) 517-00-860
Fax: (49-30) 517-00-861

International Gymnastics Hall of Fame
http://www.ighof.com

International Gymnast Magazine Online
http://www.intlgymnast.com

International Trampoline Association
http://www.itia-inc.org
3286 Stoney Ridge Road
Eugene, OR 97405
E-mail: itia@itia-inc.org
Telephone: (541) 984-0332
Fax: (541) 342-5574

USA Gymnastics
http://www.usa-gymnastics.org
Pan American Plaza
Suite 300
201 South Capitol Avenue
Indianapolis, IN 46225
E-mail: rebound@usa-gymnastics.org
Telephone: (317) 237-5050
Fax: (317) 237-5069

World Cheerleading Association
http://www.cheerwca.com
PO Box 220098
St. Louis, MO 63122
E-mail: customerservice@cheerwca.com
Telephone: (888) TEAM-WCA
Fax: (636) 498-5666

FURTHER READING

Bott, Joan. *Rhythmic Gymnastics: The Skills of the Game.* Ramsbury, U.K.: Crowood Press, 1995.

Feldman, Jane. *I Am a Gymnast.* New York: Random House, 2000.

French, Stephanie Breaux. *The Cheerleading Book.* New York: McGraw Hill/Contemporary Books, 1995.

Gymnastics Golden Moments (video). Entertainment Software, 2000.

Jackman, Joan, and Shannon Miller. *Superguides: Gymnastics.* New York: DK Publishing, 2000.

Jastrjembskaia, Nadejda, and Yuri Titov. *Rhythmic Gymnastics.* Champaign, Ill.: Human Kinetics, 1998.

McElroy, James T. *We've Got Spirit: The Life and Times of America's Greatest Cheerleading Team.* New York: Berkeley Publishing Group, 2000.

Palmer, Heather C. *Teaching Rhythmic Gymnastics: A Developmentally Appropriate Approach.* Champaign, Ill.: Human Kinetics, 2003.

Schlegel, Elfi, and Claire Ross Dunn. *The Gymnastics Book: The Young Performer's Guide to Gymnastics.* Westport, Conn.: Firefly Books, 2001.

Scott, Kieran. *Ultimate Cheerleading.* New York: Apple, 1998.

USA Gymnastics. *I Can Do Gymnastics: Essential Skills for Intermediate Gymnasts.* New York: McGraw-Hill/Contemporary Books, 1993.

Vidmar, Peter, and Karen Cogan. *Sports Psychology Library: Gymnastics.* Morgantown, W.Va.: Fitness Information Technology, 2000.

INDEX

Boldface page numbers denote major treatment of a topic. Those in *italics* denote illustrations.

A

B

T